GED
Skill Workbook Series

Mathematics 1

New Readers Press

C O N T E N T S

GED® Skill Workbook
Mathematics 1
ISBN 978-1-56420-511-7

Copyright © 2005 Trian Publishing Company
Distributed by New Readers Press
ProLiteracy's Publishing Division
1320 Jamesville Avenue, Syracuse, New York 13210
www.newreaderspress.com

Printed in the United States of America
9 8 7 6 5

Proceeds from the sale of New Readers Press materials support professional
development, training, and technical assistance programs of ProLiteracy
that benefit local literacy programs in the U.S. and around the globe.

Project Developer: Caren Van Slyke
Writer: Pamela Halloran
Editor: Jody Lynn Levine
Project Manager: Kathy Osmus
Copy Editor: Karen Schenkenfelder
Production: Jean Farley Brown
Art and Design: Karen Blanchard
Cover Design: Kimbrly Koennecke

Congratulations. You are studying to take the GED Tests in order to earn your high school equivalency certificate.

Since there is a lot of ground to cover in preparing for the test, we thought that we could help you by developing this *GED Skill* workbook series. The formula for GED success is as simple as *1–2–3*.

1. Evaluate, pages iv–11

In school and in your GED class, you have studied much of what you need to know to pass the GED. You may be asking yourself, *What do I already know? What do I need to learn? What do the GED questions look like?*

In Part 1 of this book, you will take an inventory that will help you figure out where you are in your studies. After you check your answers, you will use the *Diagnostic Chart* to target your efforts so that you can work most effectively to pass the test.

Some of the questions will check your skills; some will determine your abilities with the types of questions that you will encounter on the actual GED. In Parts 2 and 3, you will have a chance to review and practice what you need to know to pass the test.

2. Review, pages 12–63

Once you have taken the inventory, you can decide which topics you need to review. You may want to select lessons based on the *Diagnostic Chart* or work through the entire section of the book.

Part 2 of this book consists of 26 skill lessons. Each lesson has two parts:

* Skill Review
* Skill Practice

3. Practice, pages 64–83

Once you feel that you have covered the skills, the next step is to practice answering the types of questions that you will find on the GED Tests.

Part 3 of this book consists of *GED Skill Builder* lessons. These five lessons will review the types of questions that you will see on the actual test. These lessons have three parts:

* Sample Question and Think It Through
* Guided Practice
* GED Practice

Be sure that you use the hints in this part of the book. They will help you to think like a successful GED test-taker.

Best of luck,
The GED Skill Workbook Team

Evaluation

This pretest will help you learn which skills you know well and which skills you need to work on. Answer all of the questions that you can. Write your work in the space provided. Then check your answers on page 9, and use the Diagnostic Chart to analyze the results.

Number and Operations Review

Arrange the numbers in order as indicated.

1. from least to greatest

46, 42, 41, 45

3. from shortest to longest

25 in., 26 in., 23 in., 29 in.

2. from greatest to least

105, 120, 152, 125

4. from greatest to least

2,193; 2,175; 2,198; 2,189

Estimate the sum or difference as indicated.

5. Round to the hundreds place.

6,421 + 2,031

6. Use front-end estimation.

65,476 − 23,942

Solve each problem. Then choose the best answer.

7. A musical ran for 5 days at the Starlight Theater. The table shows the number of tickets sold for each performance. Rounding to the nearest thousand, about how many tickets were sold in all during the 5-day period?

Day	Tickets Sold
Wednesday	3,292
Thursday	3,621
Friday	4,075
Saturday	4,100
Sunday	3,865

(1) 20,000
(2) 19,000
(3) 18,000
(4) 17,000
(5) 16,000

8. Each choice shows the price a company charges to install the same pool. Which company has the lowest price?

(1) Ace Pools $18,300
(2) Water Works $18,398
(3) Sparkle Pools $18,500
(4) Pool Construction $18,450
(5) R. D. Pools $18,150

9. An auto mechanic did two repairs, which cost $389 and $454. About how much did both jobs cost?

(1) $400
(2) $500
(3) $600
(4) $900
(5) $1,000

Decimal Review

Arrange the numbers in order as indicated.

10. from least to greatest

    4.6, 4.62, 4.26, 4.29

11. from greatest to least

    0.34, 0.43, 0.304, 0.403

Add or subtract.

12. $11.4 + 4.62 + 6.8 =$

13. $83.145 - 15.8 =$

Multiply or divide.

14. $\begin{array}{r} 2.4 \\ \times\ 0.5 \\ \hline \end{array}$

15. $0.03\overline{)0.1062}$

Questions 16 and 17 refer to the diagram below. Solve each problem. Then fill in your answer in the grid provided.

16. The diagram below shows approximately how many Earth years it takes some of the planets to orbit the sun. How many more years does it take Saturn to orbit the sun than Jupiter?

17. Find the planet with the orbit time closest to that of Earth. What is the difference between this orbit time and Earth's orbit time?

Earth Years to Orbit Sun		
●	Venus	0.616 year
●	Earth	1 year
·	Mars	1.88 years
⬤	Jupiter	11.9 years
♄	Saturn	29.5 years

Fraction and Ratio Review

Change the mixed number to an improper fraction and the improper fraction to a mixed number.

18. $3\frac{1}{5}$

19. $\frac{15}{4}$

Find the equivalent fraction.

20. $\frac{1}{8} = \frac{}{40}$

21. $\frac{7}{10} = \frac{}{50}$

Change the fraction to a decimal and the decimal to a fraction.

22.

$\frac{4}{5}$ of Test Group Report Positive Results

$\frac{4}{5} =$

23.

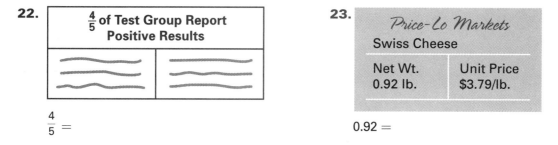

Price-Lo Markets

Swiss Cheese

Net Wt. 0.92 lb.	Unit Price $3.79/lb.

$0.92 =$

Solve each problem. For question 24, fill in your answer in the grid. You may use a calculator for question 25.

24. Meredith is making the spice mix. The only measuring spoon she can find is $\frac{1}{4}$ teaspoon. How many $\frac{1}{4}$-teaspoons of ginger should she use for the recipe?

Spice Mixture

$\frac{2}{3}$ tsp.	allspice
$\frac{1}{2}$ tsp.	ginger
$\frac{1}{4}$ tsp.	cloves
$\frac{1}{4}$ tsp.	salt

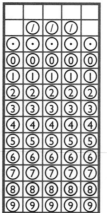

25. The Hawks football team has 60 players. Of those 60 players, 42 players are over 6 feet tall. What portion of the players are over 6 feet tall?

(1) 0.75
(2) 0.70
(3) 0.14
(4) 0.10
(5) 0.07

Solve as indicated. Reduce each answer to lowest terms.

26. $\dfrac{3}{5} + \dfrac{1}{10} =$

30. $\dfrac{1}{5}$ of $\dfrac{5}{6}$

34. $\dfrac{3}{8} + \dfrac{1}{4} + \dfrac{1}{2} =$

27. $11\dfrac{1}{2}$
$-\ 7\dfrac{7}{8}$

31. $8\dfrac{7}{10} \div 3 =$

35. $9\dfrac{2}{5}$
$-\ 5\dfrac{7}{10}$

28. $\dfrac{5}{6} - \dfrac{1}{12} =$

32. $\dfrac{7}{8} \times 5\dfrac{1}{3} =$

36. $\dfrac{3}{8} + \dfrac{1}{6} + \dfrac{2}{3} =$

29. $3\dfrac{3}{8} \div \dfrac{3}{4} =$

33. $2\dfrac{1}{3} \times 1\dfrac{3}{8} =$

37. $15 \div \dfrac{5}{8} =$

Use a calculator to solve each problem. Then choose the best answer.

38. The sign below appears on Interstate 5 in Center City. How many miles is the distance between Exit 5 and Exit 8?

(1) $2\dfrac{7}{10}$

(2) 2

(3) $1\dfrac{17}{20}$

(4) $1\dfrac{1}{4}$

(5) $\dfrac{3}{4}$

Center City Exits	
Exit 5	$\dfrac{1}{4}$ mile
Exit 6	1 mile
Exit 7	$1\dfrac{1}{2}$ miles
Exit 8	$2\dfrac{1}{10}$ miles

39. A jeweler shortens a 16-inch necklace by $1\dfrac{1}{4}$ inches. How many inches is the new length of the necklace?

(1) $13\dfrac{1}{4}$

(2) $14\dfrac{3}{4}$

(3) $15\dfrac{1}{2}$

(4) $15\dfrac{3}{4}$

(5) $17\dfrac{1}{4}$

40. Eric sets aside $\dfrac{1}{4}$ of his weekly paycheck for rent and $\dfrac{1}{8}$ of the check for food. What fraction of his weekly pay does Eric set aside for rent and food?

(1) $\dfrac{1}{32}$

(2) $\dfrac{1}{12}$

(3) $\dfrac{1}{6}$

(4) $\dfrac{1}{4}$

(5) $\dfrac{3}{8}$

41. Terri is buying fabric to make a quilt. If she buys the remnants shown below, how many yards of fabric will Terri have?

(1) $1\dfrac{13}{24}$

(2) $1\dfrac{11}{12}$

(3) $2\dfrac{1}{8}$

(4) $2\dfrac{19}{24}$

(5) $4\dfrac{7}{24}$

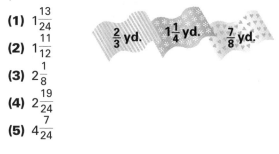

$\dfrac{2}{3}$ yd. $1\dfrac{1}{4}$ yd. $\dfrac{7}{8}$ yd.

Write each ratio as a fraction in lowest terms.

42. $120 to $54

43. 10 girls to 8 boys

44. 5 feet to 20 feet

Solve for the missing term.

45. $\dfrac{2}{10} = \dfrac{x}{100}$

46. $\dfrac{12}{5} = \dfrac{y}{60}$

47. $\dfrac{4}{5} = \dfrac{32}{t}$

Solve each problem. For question 49, fill in your answer in the grid.

48. Toni measures the distance from Lakewood to Oakhurst on the map. The distance is $\dfrac{7}{8}$ inch. Which expression shows how to find the actual distance from Lakewood to Oakhurst?

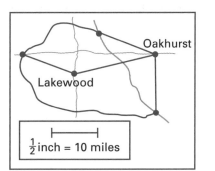

$\frac{1}{2}$ inch = 10 miles

(1) $x = \dfrac{7}{8} \times 10$

(2) $x = \dfrac{1}{2} \times 10$

(3) $\dfrac{\frac{7}{8}}{10} = \dfrac{\frac{1}{2}}{x}$

(4) $\dfrac{\frac{1}{2}}{10} = \dfrac{x}{\frac{7}{8}}$

(5) $\dfrac{\frac{1}{2}}{10} = \dfrac{\frac{7}{8}}{x}$

49. Look at the sheet of stamps below. What is the ratio of star stamps to flag stamps on the sheet? Express as a fraction in lowest terms.

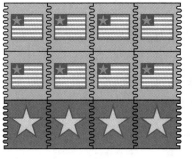

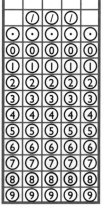

Solve.

50. Find 40% of 225.

52. 56% of what number is 1,568?

51. What percent of 500 is 300?

53. 318 is 150% of what number?

Find the percent of increase or decrease.

R.J. DAVIDSON CORPORATION

To: All Employees
From: Sales Manager

I am proud to report that our sales for this month were $24,000. Last month's sales were $20,000.

54. This month's sales to last month's sales

_____

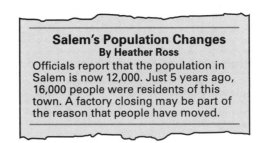

Salem's Population Changes
By Heather Ross
Officials report that the population in Salem is now 12,000. Just 5 years ago, 16,000 people were residents of this town. A factory closing may be part of the reason that people have moved.

55. Population today to population 5 years ago

_____

Solve each problem. Then choose the best answer.

56. Autumn Orchards grows five different varieties of apples. The chart shows the number of trees the orchard has for each variety. What percent of the total number of trees are McIntosh?

Variety of Apple	Number of Trees
Cortland	9
McIntosh	16
Red Delicious	10
Empire	8
Rome	7

(1) 32%
(2) 18%
(3) 16%
(4) 10%
(5) 9%

57. The ad below shows the price change for a couch. What is the rate of change in price from last week to this week?

Furniture Prices Slashed This Week!

Last Week	This Week
$400	$350

(1) 50% increase
(2) 50% decrease
(3) 14.3% decrease
(4) 12.5% increase
(5) 12.5% decrease

Questions 58 through 60 refer to the table below.

Subject	Course Number	Time	Room	Teacher
English	110	8:00–8:50	219	Farley
Math	310	8:55–9:45	115	Merrill
History	210	9:50–10:40	205	Costa
Science	510	10:45–11:35	117	Martin
Lunch		11:40–12:30	Cafeteria	

58. What time does the lunch period end?

59. What is the name of the math teacher?

60. What class meets in room 205?

Find the mean, median, and mode for each group of numbers.

61. 50, 50, 80, 60, 60, 60, 70, 70

62. 216, 218, 225, 219, 222, 212, 228

63. 1,000; 1,300; 1,100; 1,200; 1,100

Questions 64 and 65 refer to the frequency table. For questions 65 and 66, fill in your answers in the grids.

Reservations at Slopeside Hotel 1/23	
Kind of Room	**Rooms Reserved**
Standard	𝍷𝍷𝍷𝍷 𝍷𝍷𝍷𝍷 𝍷𝍷𝍷𝍷 𝍷𝍷𝍷𝍷 ////
Deluxe	𝍷𝍷𝍷𝍷 𝍷𝍷𝍷𝍷 𝍷𝍷𝍷𝍷 ///
Studio	𝍷𝍷𝍷𝍷 𝍷𝍷𝍷𝍷 //
Suite	𝍷𝍷𝍷𝍷 ///

66. Sean is a lacrosse goalie. The table shows the number of saves he made in his first five games. What is his *mean* number of saves?

Game	1	2	3	4	5
Saves	12	15	16	10	12

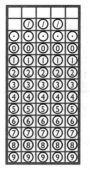

64. The Slopeside Hotel has a total of 80 rooms. What percent of the total rooms are reserved for this night?

(1) 80%
(2) 77.5%
(3) 67.5%
(4) 62%
(5) 22.5%

65. How many studios and suites are reserved for this night?

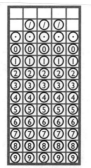

Questions 67 and 68 refer to the line graph below.

The line graph shows how much Edward earned in 4 months plowing driveways.

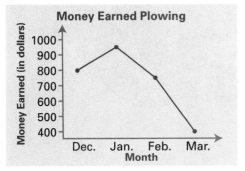

67. How much more did Edward earn in January than in March?

68. Between which two months was there a difference in earnings of $200?

Questions 69 and 70 refer to the bar graph below.

The bar graph shows the number of seniors who have different majors at Carey College.

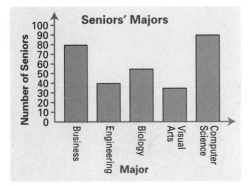

69. Computer science majors make up what percent of the senior class?

70. How many more seniors major in biology than in visual arts?

Solve each problem. Then choose the best answer.

71. Which of these phrases best describes the correlation in the scatter plot?

   (1) negative correlation, weak
   (2) negative correlation, strong
   (3) positive correlation, weak
   (4) positive correlation, strong
   (5) Not enough information is given.

72. What would you predict would be the average shoe size of a boy about 61 inches tall?

   (1) 4
   (2) 5
   (3) 6
   (4) 7
   (5) Not enough information is given.

The scatter plot shows the height and corresponding shoe size of ten teenage boys.

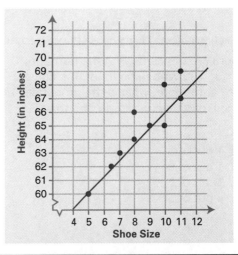

Questions 73 and 74 refer to the graph below.

73. Trucks and cars are what percent of sales at Ace's Auto Sales?

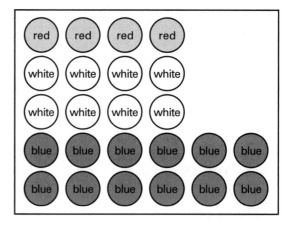

Ace's Auto Sales

Trucks **12%**
Cars **42%**
SUV **19%**
Vans **27%**

74. If Ace's sold 1,000 vehicles, how many would you predict would be vans?

Find the experimental probability.

Susan rolled two number cubes 100 times and recorded each sum. The results are shown in the table below.

Sum	2	3	4	5	6	7	8	9	10	11	12
Times Rolled	1	6	9	12	13	18	12	10	8	7	4

75. What is the probability of rolling an 11 or a 12?

76. What is the probability of rolling a 6, a 7, or an 8?

Use the illustration of a box of chips to solve each question.

77. Tara picks a blue chip and holds onto it. Then she picks another chip. What is the probability that the second chip is also blue?

78. Kevin picks a white chip and then puts it back in the box. If he picks a second chip, what is the probability that it is also white?

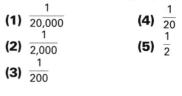

red red red red
white white white white
white white white white
blue blue blue blue blue blue
blue blue blue blue blue blue

Solve each problem. Then choose the correct answer.

79. There are ten cards with the numbers 1 through 10 written on them. If a player picks a card at random, what is the probability that he or she picks a number greater than 8?

(1) 1 out of 10
(2) 1 out of 8
(3) 1 out of 6
(4) 1 out of 5
(5) 4 out of 5

80. If a customer picks a black marble out of a jar, he or she wins a prize. If there are 1,000 marbles and 5 are black, what is the probability of winning a prize?

(1) $\frac{1}{20,000}$ **(4)** $\frac{1}{20}$

(2) $\frac{1}{2,000}$ **(5)** $\frac{1}{2}$

(3) $\frac{1}{200}$

Answers and explanations start on page 9.

1. 41, 42, 45, 46
2. 152, 125, 120, 105
3. 23 in., 25 in., 26 in., 29 in.
4. 2,198; 2,193; 2,189; 2,175
5. 8,400
6. 40,000
7. **(2) 19,000** Round each number to the thousands place and then add: $3{,}000 + 4{,}000 + 4{,}000 + 4{,}000 + 4{,}000 = 19{,}000$.
8. **(5) R. D. Pools $18,150** Compare the numbers. Since all numbers have the same digits in the ten thousands and thousands place, look at the hundreds place. The number with the least hundreds digit is 18,150.
9. **(4) $900** Round both numbers to the nearest hundred and add: $\$400 + \$500 = \$900$.

10. 4.26, 4.29, 4.6, 4.62
11. 0.43, 0.403, 0.34, 0.304
12. 22.82
13. 67.345
14. 1.2
15. 3.54
16. 17.6

17. 0.384

18. $\frac{16}{5}$

19. $3\frac{3}{4}$

20. $\frac{1}{8} = \frac{5}{40}$

21. $\frac{7}{10} = \frac{35}{50}$

22. $\frac{4}{5} = 0.8$

23. $0.92 = \frac{23}{25}$

24. 2

25. **(2) 0.70** Divide to find the portion of the total: $42 \div 60 = 0.7$.

26. $\frac{7}{10}$

27. $3\frac{5}{8}$

28. $\frac{3}{4}$

29. $4\frac{1}{2}$

30. $\frac{1}{6}$

31. $2\frac{9}{10}$

32. $4\frac{2}{3}$

33. $3\frac{5}{24}$

34. $1\frac{1}{8}$

35. $3\frac{7}{10}$

36. $1\frac{5}{24}$

37. 24
38. **(3) $1\frac{17}{20}$** Subtract the distance for Exit 5 from the distance for Exit 8:
   $2\frac{1}{10} - \frac{1}{4} = 2\frac{2}{20} - \frac{5}{20}$. Then regroup $2\frac{2}{20}$ and subtract:
   $1\frac{22}{20} - \frac{5}{20} = 1\frac{17}{20}$.
39. **(2) $14\frac{3}{4}$** Subtract: $16 - 1\frac{1}{4} = 14\frac{3}{4}$.
40. **(5) $\frac{3}{8}$** Add the fractions: $\frac{1}{4} + \frac{1}{8} = \frac{3}{8}$.
41. **(4) $2\frac{19}{24}$** Add the amounts for each remnant:
   $\frac{2}{3} + 1\frac{1}{4} + \frac{7}{8} = \frac{16}{24} + 1\frac{6}{24} + \frac{21}{24} = 2\frac{19}{24}$.

42. $\frac{\$20}{\$9}$

43. $\frac{5}{4}$

44. $\frac{1}{4}$

45. $x = 20$
46. $y = 144$
47. $t = 40$

48. (5) $\dfrac{\frac{1}{2}}{10} = \dfrac{\frac{7}{8}}{x}$

This proportion states that $\frac{1}{2}$ inch is to 10 miles as $\frac{7}{8}$ is to x miles. Both ratios have the map measurement on the top and the equivalent mileage figure on the bottom.

49. **1/2** There are 4 star stamps and 8 flag stamps. The ratio of stars to flags is 4 to 8 or 4/8, which is 1/2 in lowest terms.

50. 90
51. 60%
52. 2,800
53. 212
54. 20% increase
55. 25% decrease
56. (1) **32%** First, add to find the total number of trees: $9 + 6 + 10 + 8 + 7 = 50$. Then divide the number of McIntosh trees by the total number of trees: $16 \div 50 = 0.32 = 32\%$.
57. (5) **12.5% decrease** Find the difference in the prices, and compare this to the original amount (last week's price): $\$400 - \$350 = \$50$, and $\$50 \div \$400 = 0.125 = 12.5\%$. Since the price has decreased, it is a 12.5% decrease.

58. 12:30
59. Merrill
60. History
61. mean $= 62.5$; median $= 60$; mode $= 60$
62. mean $= 220$; median $= 219$; mode $=$ none
63. mean $= 1,140$; median $= 1,100$; mode $= 1,100$
64. (2) **77.5%** Add to find the total number of rooms reserved: $24 + 18 + 12 + 8 = 62$. Then divide by the total number of rooms in the hotel: $62 \div 80 = 0.775 = 77.5\%$.
65. **20**
Add to find the total suites and studios: $12 + 8 = 20$.

66. **13**
Add the saves for each game: $12 + 15 + 16 + 10 + 12 = 65$. Then divide by the number of games: $65 \div 5 = 13$.

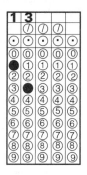

67. 550
68. January and February
69. 30%
70. 20
71. (4) **positive correlation, strong** In general, the shoe size increases as the height increases. The points are close to the fitted line, so the correlation is strong.
72. (3) **6** On the line, 61 inches is closest to a size 6. This would be the best prediction.
73. 54%
74. 270
75. $\dfrac{11}{100}$
76. $\dfrac{43}{100}$
77. $\dfrac{11}{23}$
78. $\dfrac{1}{3}$
79. (4) **1 out of 5** Two of the 10 cards in the deck are greater than 8 (9 and 10). The probability of picking one of these cards is 2 out of 10, or 1 out of 5 in lowest terms.
80. (3) $\dfrac{1}{200}$ There are 5 black marbles out of 1,000 marbles. Write a fraction and reduce: $\dfrac{5}{1,000} = \dfrac{1}{200}$.

Diagnostic Chart

1. Check your answers to the Math Skills Inventory on page 9.
2. Circle the numbers of the questions you got correct.
3. Add the number of questions you got right for each skill (across), and write the number under Total Correct.
4. Add the number of total questions you got correct (down).
5. Check off (✓) the skill areas that you feel you most need to work on.

PROBLEM NUMBERS	TOTAL CORRECT	SKILL	✓	PAGE NUMBERS
		Number and Operations		
1, 2, 3, 4	_____ / 4	Number Sense		pp. 12–13
5, 6	_____ / 2	Estimation		pp. 14–15
		Decimals		
10, 11	_____ / 2	Decimal Basics		pp. 16–17
12, 13	_____ / 2	Add and Subtract Decimals		pp. 18–19
14, 15	_____ / 2	Multiply and Divide Decimals		pp. 20–21
		Fractions and Ratios		
18, 19	_____ / 2	Fraction Basics		pp. 22–23
20, 21	_____ / 2	Equivalent Fractions		pp. 24–25
22, 23	_____ / 2	Fractions and Decimals		pp. 26–27
26, 34, 36	_____ / 3	Add Fractions		pp. 28–29
27, 28, 35	_____ / 3	Subtract Fractions		pp. 30–31
30, 32, 33	_____ / 3	Multiply Fractions		pp. 32–33
29, 31, 37	_____ / 3	Divide Fractions		pp. 34–35
42, 43, 44	_____ / 3	Ratios		pp. 36–37
45, 46, 47	_____ / 3	Proportions		pp. 38–39
		Percents		
50	_____ / 1	Solve for the Part		pp. 40–41
51	_____ / 1	Solve for the Rate		pp. 42–43
52, 53	_____ / 2	Solve for the Base		pp. 44–45
54, 55	_____ / 2	Percent of Change		pp. 46–47
		Data Analysis		
58, 59, 60	_____ / 3	Tables		pp. 48–49
61, 62, 63	_____ / 3	Mean, Median, and Mode		pp. 50–51
69, 70	_____ / 2	Bar Graphs		pp. 52–53
67, 68	_____ / 2	Line Graphs		pp. 54–55
71, 72	_____ / 2	Scatter Plots		pp. 56–57
73, 74	_____ / 2	Circle Graphs		pp. 58–59
75, 76	_____ / 2	Probability, Part I		pp. 60–61
77, 78	_____ / 2	Probability, Part II		pp. 62–63
		GED Questions		
7, 8, 9, 79, 80	_____ / 5	Word Problems		pp. 64–67
16, 17, 24, 65, 66	_____ / 5	The Standard Grid		pp. 68–71
25, 38, 39, 40, 41	_____ / 5	The Casio fx-260 Calculator		pp. 72–75
48, 56, 57, 64	_____ / 4	Problem Solving		pp. 76–79
49	_____ / 1	Fractions on the Standard Grid		pp. 80–83
TOTAL	_____ / 80			

Place Value

The value of a number depends on how many digits make up the number and on the placement of the digits. Review the place-value diagram shown at the right.

You can use symbols to compare numbers.

Millions   Hundred Thousands   Ten Thousands   Thousands   Hundreds   Tens   Ones

— , — — — , — — —

$=$ means *is equal to*
$<$ means *is less than*
$\leq$ means *is less than or equal to*
$>$ means *is greater than*
$\geq$ means *is greater than or equal to*

Comparing Numbers

To compare whole numbers, first look to see if they have the same number of digits. The number with the most digits is the greater number.

Compare 8,679 and 10,205. Count the number of digits in each number.

10,205 ◄—— five digits
8,679   ◄—— four digits   **10,205 $>$ 8,679** because 10,205 has more digits than 8,679.

If the whole numbers have the same number of digits, work from left to right, comparing place values until the digits are different.

Compare 1,058 and 1,073. Since both numbers have four digits, start by comparing the thousands place.

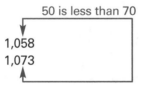

50 is less than 70

1,058
1,073

Since 50 is less than 70, **1,058 $<$ 1,073.**

Grouping and Ordering

Grouping numbers requires you to place numbers in categories.

Out of 436, 558, 550, and 289, which amounts belong in the group $x \leq 550$?

The amounts **436, 550, and 289** make $x \leq 550$ true.

Ordering means arranging amounts in order according to value.

Place the amounts 436, 550, and 289 in order from least to greatest. In order from least to greatest: **289, 436, and 550.**

Number and Operations Practice 1

A. Write <, =, or > to make each statement true.

1. 85 _____ 83

2. 22 _____ 55

3. 104 _____ 110

4. 240 _____ 303

5. 1,476 _____ 1,476

6. 5,213 _____ 4,768

7. 12,242 _____ 11,422

8. 67,809 _____ 67,908

9. 250,000 _____ 255,000

B. Arrange the numbers in order as directed.

10. least to greatest: 25, 28, 23, 29

11. greatest to least: 105, 120, 152, 125

12. lightest to heaviest: 15 lb., 12 lb., 19 lb.

13. greatest to least: 5,048; 5,277; 5,008

C. Out of the numbers 1 through 150, choose the numbers that make each statement true.

14. Which numbers belong in the group $x < 58$?

15. Which numbers belong in the group $93 \leq x \leq 150$?

16. Which numbers belong in the group $101 \leq x \leq 105$?

D. Solve each problem. Then choose the correct answer.

17. List the boxes in order from heaviest to lightest in weight.

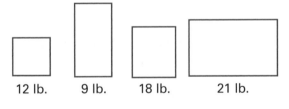

12 lb.   9 lb.   18 lb.   21 lb.

(1) 9 lb., 12 lb., 18 lb., 21 lb.
(2) 12 lb., 9 lb., 18 lb., 21 lb.
(3) 12 lb., 18 lb., 21 lb, 9 lb.
(4) 21 lb., 18 lb., 12 lb., 9 lb.
(5) 21 lb., 12 lb., 18 lb., 9 lb.

18. A horse show offers a class to riders between the ages of 18 and 39. Which age below can enter the class?

(1) 13
(2) 17
(3) 35
(4) 40
(5) 45

19. A shipping company has a special price for packages heavier than 150 pounds but lighter than 300 pounds. Which whole numbers belong in the group $150 < x < 300$?

(1) $x = 1$ through 149
(2) $x = 150$ through 299
(3) $x = 150$ through 300
(4) $x = 151$ through 299
(5) $x = 300$ through 500

20. On which day was the greatest number of concert tickets sold?

(1) Day 1—8,672 tickets
(2) Day 2—8,243 tickets
(3) Day 3—8,746 tickets
(4) Day 4—8,731 tickets
(5) Day 5—8,167 tickets

Answers and explanations start on page 84.

Rounding

Estimation can be used to get an approximate answer for a calculation. Use estimation when you do not need to find an exact answer. Estimation can also help you decide if an answer is reasonable.

Rounding makes numbers easier to work with.

Round these numbers to the nearest thousand, then add.

22,562 + 36,324

1. Circle the digit you want to round to.
2. Underline the digit to the right.
3. If the underlined digit is greater than or equal to 5, round up. Add 1 to the circled digit. If the underlined digit is less than 5, round down. Do not change the circled digit.

22,562 rounds up to 23,000.

36,324 rounds down to 36,000.

Add: 23,000 + 36,000 = 59,000
The sum of 22,562 and 36,324 is approximately **59,000.**

Front-end Estimation

You can also use front-end estimation to find an approximate answer. Estimate with the front digits, which are the digits with the greatest place value.

$$
\begin{array}{r}
5{,}688 \\
-\ 2{,}357 \\
\end{array}
\quad
\begin{array}{r}
\text{is approximately}\ 5{,}000 \\
-\ 2{,}000 \\
\hline
\mathbf{3{,}000}
\end{array}
$$

Front-end estimation can be faster than rounding, but often rounding provides a closer answer.

ROUNDING
Round to the nearest thousand. Then add.

33,750 + 45,482

Round 33,750 to 34,000.
Round 45,482 to 45,000.

34,000 + 45,000 = 79,000

FRONT-END ESTIMATION
Use the front digits to estimate the sum.

33,750 + 45,482

33,750 + 45,482

30,000 + 40,000 = 70,000

Compare the estimates to the actual sum.   33,750 + 45,482 = 79,232

The rounding estimate is closer to the actual sum.

Number and Operations Practice 2

A. Round the numbers as directed.

1. Round 63,468 to the thousands place.

2. Round 4,692 to the hundreds place.

3. Round 8,794 to the thousands place.

4. Round 435,969 to the ten thousands place.

5. Round 5,202,478 to the millions place.

6. Round 33,668 to the ten thousands place.

7. Round 174,985 to the thousands place.

8. Round 864 to the tens place.

B. Estimate the sum or difference as directed.

9. Round to the hundreds place.

   $3,069 + 3,412$

10. Use front-end estimation.

    $3,202,000 + 5,452,000$

11. Round to the ten thousands place.

    $256,086 - 104,854$

12. Use front-end estimation.

    $42,890 + 47,403$

13. Use front-end estimation.

    $579 - 496$

14. Round to the thousands place.

    $62,865 - 12,365$

C. Solve each problem. Then choose the correct answer.

15. Tomas priced a new car at $16,865. What is this amount rounded to the nearest thousand?

    (1) $16,000
    (2) $16,800
    (3) $16,900
    (4) $17,000
    (5) $20,000

16. Tad paid $568 for telephone service, $739 for cable TV, and $486 for Internet service. Using front-end estimation, about how much did he spend for all three services?

    (1) $1,500
    (2) $1,600
    (3) $1,700
    (4) $1,800
    (5) $1,900

17. About how much more water was pumped from Well 2 than from Well 1? Round to the millions place.

Gallons of Water Pumped	
Well 1	62,360,750
Well 2	95,704,000

    (1) 34,000,000
    (2) 33,000,000
    (3) 32,000,000
    (4) 30,000,000
    (5) 3,400,000

Answers and explanations start on page 84.

Place Value

A decimal number is a way to express a quantity less than one. Decimals, like whole numbers, can be shown in a place-value chart.

As you move to the left in a decimal number, the values increase. As you move to the right, the values decrease.

The number in the chart has a whole number part and a decimal part. To name the decimal, find the place value of the last digit on the right. In this decimal, it is the hundredths place. The decimal 3.46 is read *three <u>and</u> forty-six hundredths.*

Placeholder Zeros

In some numbers, there are decimal places that have no values. In these numbers, a placeholder zero is used.

0.08   Read as *eight hundredths.*
0.054   Read as *fifty-four thousandths.*

Comparing and Ordering

Which is greater, $0.63 or $0.65? You know $0.65 is the greater amount. These two decimals have the same number of places. How do you compare decimals when the number of places is different?

Compare 0.81 and 0.805. Add 0 to the thousandths place so the decimals have the same number of places.

0.810   Adding a zero to the end of a decimal number does not change the value of the decimal.
0.805

Think of the decimal digits as whole numbers: 810 > 805, so **0.81 > 0.805.**

You can also compare mixed decimals. Be sure to compare the whole numbers first. Then compare the decimal place values, if necessary.

Compare 21.985 and 22.03.

21.985
22.03

Compare the whole numbers first: 21 < 22, so **21.985 < 22.03.**

Like whole numbers, decimals can be ordered by value. These decimals are shown in order from least to greatest: 0.0068, 0.0092, 0.0150.

Decimal Review Practice 1

A. Write numbers for words. Express numbers in word form.

1. two and five hundredths

3. 5.0008

5. fifteen and six tenths

2. one hundred two thousandths

4. 0.3945

6. 0.0495

B. Write <, =, or > to make each statement true.

7. 0.62 _____ 0.604

9. 0.512 _____ 0.215

11. 0.898 _____ 0.988

8. 32.05 _____ 34.92

10. 3.1 _____ 3.10

12. 56.079 _____ 59.607

C. Arrange the numbers in order as directed.

13. least to greatest: 2.5, 2.48, 2.35, 2.39

15. lightest to heaviest: 8.05 g, 8.5 g, 7.2 g

14. greatest to least: 0.003, 0.30, 0.03, 3.0

16. greatest to least: 0.12, 0.21, 0.102

D. Solve each problem. Then choose the correct answer.

17. Ari estimates that his groceries will cost between $18.00 and $20.00. If his estimate is accurate, which amount shows a possible total of his grocery bill?

(1) $16.50
(2) $17.98
(3) $19.79
(4) $20.02
(5) $21.00

18. How would you read 3.48?

(1) thirty-four and eight tenths
(2) three and forty-eight hundredths
(3) three and four hundred eight thousandths
(4) three and four tenths
(5) three hundred forty-eight thousandths

19. Earthquakes are measured using the Richter scale. Based on the strength of the earthquakes, list the years in order from weakest to strongest earthquake.

Date of Earthquake	Richter Scale
1920	8.6
1923	8.3
1939	7.9
1976	8.0

(1) 1920, 1923, 1976, 1939
(2) 1939, 1976, 1920, 1923
(3) 1976, 1939, 1923, 1920
(4) 1939, 1976, 1923, 1920
(5) 1939, 1923, 1976, 1920

Answers and explanations start on page 84.

Addition

Like whole numbers, decimals can be added. Many situations involving money call for addition with decimals.

The sales tax for the television set pictured below is $21.45. What is the total cost of the television set with tax?

$429

1. To add, first line up the decimal points. Insert placeholder zeros if necessary.

$$\begin{array}{r} \$429.00 \\ +\ \ 21.45 \\ \hline \end{array}$$

2. Next, add as you would with whole numbers. Regroup as needed.

3. Be sure to bring the decimal point directly down into the answer.

$$\begin{array}{r} \$429.00 \\ +\ \ 21.45 \\ \hline \$450.45 \end{array}$$

The total cost of the television with tax is **$450.45.**

Subtraction

Some problems with decimals require subtraction. You should set up decimal subtraction problems the same way you did with addition problems.

This graph shows the substances that make up seawater. What is the difference between the percentages of sodium and chloride?

Seawater

Chloride 54.3%

Sodium 30.2%

Other 4.2%

Magnesium 3.7%

Sulfate 7.6%

1. To subtract, line up the decimal points. Add placeholder zeros if necessary.

$$\begin{array}{r} 54.3 \\ -\ 30.2 \\ \hline \end{array}$$

2. Next, subtract as you would with whole numbers. Regroup as needed.

3. Be sure to bring the decimal point directly down into the answer.

$$\begin{array}{r} 54.3 \\ -\ 30.2 \\ \hline 24.1 \end{array}$$

The difference between the percentages of sodium and chloride is **24.1.**

Decimal Review Practice 2

A. Add or subtract.

1. $1.03
      +$0.62

4. 4.095
       − 2.352

7. 62.346
       + 4.07

2. 0.76
       + 3.048

5. 3,883.9
       − 73.12

8. 28.903
       +5.18

3. $45.32
       + $20.03

6. 8.072
       + 0.25

9. 7.642
       − 3.903

B. Add or subtract. Be sure to line up the decimal points.

10. 15.3 + 2.45 + 8.6 =

12. 60.333 − 12.4 =

11. 92.5 − 8.125 =

13. $253.10 + $6.05 + $0.90 =

C. Solve each problem. Then choose the correct answer.

14. The table shows four swimmers' times in a race. What is the difference, in seconds, between the fastest and slowest times?

Swimmer	Time (in seconds)
Rocha	58.62
Hanes	55.04
Chung	59.10
Thompson	56.56

(1) 1.52
(2) 2.54
(3) 4.06
(4) 4.16
(5) 5.06

15. In the next race, Thompson took 0.8 second off his time. What was his time, in seconds, in this race?

(1) 57.36
(2) 56.76
(3) 56.48
(4) 55.76
(5) 54.76

16. Janice buys a drill for $89.95, a sander for $74.95, and an extension cord for $12.95. How much does she spend in all?

(1) $164.90
(2) $176.85
(3) $176.95
(4) $177.75
(5) $177.85

17. Lina's jogging route is 8.25 miles long. She has already jogged 5.8 miles. How many more miles does Lina have to jog?

(1) 2.45
(2) 2.55
(3) 3.17
(4) 3.45
(5) 14.05

Answers and explanations start on page 84.

Multiplication

Decimals can be multiplied by whole numbers and by other decimals. The procedure for multiplication of decimals is the same as multiplication with whole numbers. The key difference is the placement of the decimal point.

A telephone plan charges $0.08 per minute for long-distance calls. What would the charge be for 162 long-distance minutes?

To solve this problem, multiply the number of minutes by the cost per minute.

1. Set up the problem. Line up the digits and ignore the decimal point. Multiply as you would with whole numbers.

$$\begin{array}{r} ^{4\,1}162 \\ \times\ 0.08 \\ \hline 1296 \end{array}$$

2. Count the number of decimal places in both factors.

162   0 places
0.08   2 places

3. Count 2 places from the right in the product, and insert the decimal point.

12.96

The charge for long-distance minutes is **$12.96.**

Division

Some division problems have a whole-number divisor, and others have a decimal divisor.

1. With whole-number divisors, first place the decimal point in the quotient above the decimal in the dividend.

$64\overline{)2.88}$

2. Next, divide as you would with whole numbers.

$$\begin{array}{r} .045 \\ 64\overline{)2.880} \\ -2\,56 \\ \hline 320 \\ -320 \\ \hline 0 \end{array}$$

1. With decimal divisors, first move the decimal point the same number of places in the divisor and dividend to make a whole-number divisor.

$0.03\overline{)12.00.}$

2. Next, put the decimal point in the quotient right above the decimal point in the dividend. Then divide.

$$\begin{array}{r} 400. \\ 3\overline{)1200.} \\ -12 \\ \hline 0 \end{array}$$

Decimal Review Practice 3

A. Multiply or divide.

1. $\begin{array}{r} 3.6 \\ \times\ 0.8 \\ \hline \end{array}$

3. $\begin{array}{r} 23.02 \\ \times\ 3.18 \\ \hline \end{array}$

5. $11.5\overline{)23.0805}$

2. $1.9\overline{)6.08}$

4. $0.06\overline{)8.28}$

6. $\begin{array}{r} 7.02 \\ \times\ 2.74 \\ \hline \end{array}$

B. Multiply or divide. Be sure to line up the digits.

7. $5.75 \div 115$

9. 0.007×21.9

11. 52.75×6

8. 1.89×62

10. $0.09\overline{)3.834}$

12. $0.4\overline{)5.556}$

C. Solve each problem. Then choose the correct answer.

13. Hillary wants to compare the prices of two different brands of ketchup. To do this, she finds the price per ounce. What is the price per ounce for this bottle of ketchup? (Hint: Divide the price by the number of ounces.)

(1) $0.005
(2) $0.05
(3) $0.50
(4) $5.00
(5) $64.80

14. In the summer, Clark paddles his kayak 4.25 miles each day, 5 days a week. How many miles does Clark paddle in 1 week?

(1)   0.85
(2)   2.125
(3) 20.05
(4) 21.25
(5) 212.5

15. Baseballs have a diameter of about 5.25 inches. A box is 42 inches wide. How many baseballs will fit in a row inside the box?

(1)   0.8
(2)   7
(3)   8
(4) 80
(5) 220

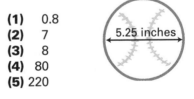

5.25 inches

16. Chicken breasts are on sale for $2.79 per pound. What is the price for a pack of chicken breasts that weighs 4.28 pounds? Round the answer to the nearest cent.

(1) $1.19
(2) $9.47
(3) $11.84
(4) $11.94
(5) $12.94

Answers and explanations start on page 84.

Understanding Fractions

A fraction is used to show equal parts of a whole or of a group. In the model for $\frac{3}{4}$, the rectangle is divided into four equal parts.

$\frac{3}{4}$ 3 numerator (number shaded)
4 denominator (number of equal parts)

$\frac{9}{6}$ 9 numerator (number shaded)
6 denominator (number of equal parts)

The numerator shows the number of parts shaded. The denominator shows the total number of equal parts in the whole.

A proper fraction shows a quantity less than 1. The numerator is less than the denominator. An improper fraction shows a quantity greater than or equal to 1. The numerator is greater than or equal to the denominator.

Mixed Numbers

A mixed number shows a quantity greater than 1 by using a whole number and a fraction. In the model above for $\frac{9}{6}$, the shaded area combines one whole rectangle and 3 out of 6 parts of the second rectangle. The fraction $\frac{9}{6}$ can be written as the mixed number $1\frac{3}{6}$, or $1\frac{1}{2}$.

You can change an improper fraction to a mixed number or change a mixed number to an improper fraction.

Change $\frac{12}{5}$ to a mixed number.

Note: The fraction bar means *divide*. Divide 12 by 5.

$$\begin{array}{r} 2 \\ 5\overline{)12} \\ -10 \\ \hline 2 \end{array}$$

Write the remainder as a fraction with the original denominator.

$$\frac{12}{5} = 2\frac{2}{5}$$

Change $2\frac{2}{5}$ to an improper fraction.

Multiply the whole number by the denominator, and then add the numerator. The denominator stays the same.

$$2\frac{2}{5} = \frac{2 \times 5 + 2}{5} = \frac{12}{5}$$

Comparing Fractions

It is easy to compare like fractions, or fractions with a common denominator. Look at the numerators. The fraction with the greater numerator is the greater fraction.

$\frac{5}{8} > \frac{1}{8}$ Since $5 > 1$, $\frac{5}{8} > \frac{1}{8}$.

$\frac{3}{10} < \frac{7}{10}$ Since $3 < 7$, $\frac{3}{10} < \frac{7}{10}$.

Fraction and Ratio Review Practice 1

A. Write a fraction for the shaded part.

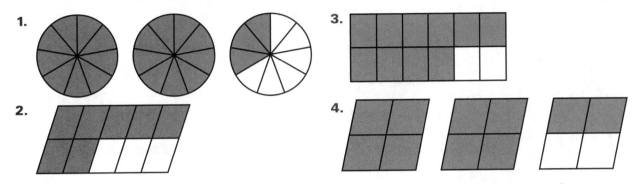

1.

2.

3.

4.

B. Change each mixed number to an improper fraction and each improper fraction to a mixed number.

5. $4\frac{3}{10}$

6. $5\frac{3}{5}$

7. $\frac{13}{4}$

8. $\frac{17}{12}$

9. $\frac{14}{3}$

10. $3\frac{5}{6}$

C. Write <, =, or > to make each statement true.

11. $\frac{7}{8}$ _____ $\frac{3}{8}$

12. $\frac{11}{12}$ _____ $\frac{17}{12}$

13. $\frac{3}{2}$ _____ $1\frac{1}{2}$

14. $\frac{3}{3}$ _____ $\frac{5}{3}$

15. $\frac{1}{6}$ _____ $\frac{5}{6}$

16. $1\frac{1}{10}$ _____ $\frac{11}{10}$

D. Solve each problem. Then choose the correct answer.

17. Rachel could find only her $\frac{1}{4}$-cup measuring cup. She filled it with milk 5 times to measure for a recipe. How many cups of milk did Rachel need?

(1) $\frac{3}{4}$

(2) 1

(3) $1\frac{1}{4}$

(4) $1\frac{3}{4}$

(5) 5

18. The lengths below are given in inches. Which is the shortest length?

(1) $1\frac{1}{8}$ **(4)** $\frac{3}{8}$

(2) $\frac{7}{8}$ **(5)** $\frac{1}{8}$

(3) $\frac{5}{8}$

19. A manager asked her employees how far they travel from home to work. The results are shown below. Which worker travels the greatest distance?

Distance Traveled to Work	
Holland	$8\frac{1}{10}$ miles
Paige	$8\frac{3}{10}$ miles
Jacob	$7\frac{9}{10}$ miles
Gomez	$8\frac{7}{10}$ miles
Chung	$8\frac{9}{10}$ miles

(1) Holland   **(4)** Gomez
(2) Paige   **(5)** Chung
(3) Jacobs

Answers and explanations start on page 85.

Reducing Fractions

Equivalent fractions are fractions that have equal value. You can use multiplication and division to find equivalent fractions. Sometimes you want to reduce a fraction so it is written in lowest terms. When a fraction is in lowest terms, there is no number other than 1 that can be divided evenly into the numerator and denominator.

Of the 10 members in a book club, 8 people live in the same neighborhood. In lowest terms, what fraction of the members lives in the same neighborhood?

1. Write a fraction.

8 out of 10 $= \dfrac{8}{10}$

2. Find the greatest common factor of both numbers: 2.

Factors of 8: 1, 2, 4, 8

3. Divide the numerator and denominator by the greatest common factor.

Factors of 10: 1, 2, 5, 10

$$\dfrac{8 \div 2}{10 \div 2} = \dfrac{4}{5}$$

In lowest terms, the fraction $\dfrac{8}{10}$ is equal to $\dfrac{4}{5}$.

Raising Fractions

There are times when you need to express a fraction in higher terms. You can raise a fraction to find an equivalent fraction.

Which fraction is greater, $\dfrac{3}{5}$ or $\dfrac{2}{3}$?

1. Find the least common denominator for both fractions. Start by finding the multiples of the greater denominator. Look for multiples of both denominators.

Multiples of 5: 5, 10, 15, 20, 25

15 is also a multiple of 3.

The least common denominator of 3 and 5 is 15.

2. Multiply to find equivalent fractions with common denominators.

$$\dfrac{3}{5} = \dfrac{?}{15} \quad \dfrac{3 \times 3}{5 \times 3} = \dfrac{9}{15} \quad \dfrac{2}{3} = \dfrac{?}{15} \quad \dfrac{2 \times 5}{3 \times 5} = \dfrac{10}{15}$$

THINK:
5 times what is 15?   3 times what is 15?

3. Now you can compare the fractions with the same denominator.

$$\dfrac{9}{15} < \dfrac{10}{15} \qquad \text{So } \dfrac{3}{5} < \dfrac{2}{3}$$

If two fractions are equivalent, the cross products are equal.

$$\dfrac{3}{5} \overset{?}{=} \dfrac{9}{15} \qquad \begin{aligned} 3 \times 5 &= 45 \\ 5 \times 9 &= 45 \end{aligned} \qquad \dfrac{3}{5} = \dfrac{9}{15}$$

Fraction and Ratio Review Practice 2

A. Reduce each fraction to lowest terms.

1. $\frac{15}{18}$

2. $\frac{9}{12}$

3. $\frac{8}{24}$

4. $\frac{4}{20}$

5. $\frac{8}{56}$

6. $\frac{16}{20}$

7. $\frac{14}{16}$

8. $\frac{10}{15}$

9. $\frac{8}{16}$

10. $\frac{12}{36}$

11. $\frac{18}{48}$

12. $\frac{21}{36}$

B. Find the equivalent fraction.

13. $\frac{1}{6} = \frac{}{36}$

14. $\frac{5}{12} = \frac{}{48}$

15. $\frac{1}{4} = \frac{}{28}$

16. $\frac{3}{5} = \frac{}{40}$

17. $\frac{5}{8} = \frac{}{32}$

18. $\frac{3}{10} = \frac{}{50}$

19. $\frac{1}{12} = \frac{}{60}$

20. $\frac{1}{9} = \frac{}{54}$

21. $\frac{7}{10} = \frac{}{30}$

C. Solve each problem. Then choose the correct answer.

22. The Monroe Company has 60 employees. Twelve of the employees take the train to work. The rest of the workers drive their cars. In lowest terms, what fraction of the employees drives to work?

(1) $\frac{1}{5}$

(2) $\frac{1}{3}$

(3) $\frac{3}{5}$

(4) $\frac{2}{3}$

(5) $\frac{4}{5}$

23. Bill scored $\frac{1}{3}$ of the points in a basketball game. Which of these could be the number of points he and the team scored in that game?

(1) 50 out of 75 points
(2) 24 out of 72 points
(3) 17 out of 68 points
(4) 20 out of 80 points
(5) 13 out of 65 points

24. Each Centerville company plans to collect $10,000 for charity. The chart below shows what fraction of this amount they have collected. Which business has collected the least amount?

Business	Fraction of Amount Collected
A	$\frac{1}{2}$
B	$\frac{3}{8}$
C	$\frac{3}{6}$
D	$\frac{5}{12}$
E	$\frac{3}{4}$

(1) Business A
(2) Business B
(3) Business C
(4) Business D
(5) Business E

Answers and explanations start on page 85.

Decimals to Fractions

Decimals and fractions both represent parts of a whole. That's why decimals and fractions can be changed from one form to the other.

Express 0.625 as a fraction.

Calculator display: 0.625

1. Read the decimal. This is the same as 625 out of 1,000.

   six hundred twenty-five thousandths

2. Write the fraction $\frac{625}{1,000}$.

   $$\frac{625 \div 125}{1,000 \div 125} = \frac{5}{8}$$

3. Reduce the fraction to lowest terms.

Notice that the numerator of the fraction is equal to the decimal without the decimal point. The denominator is the place value of the last digit of the decimal.

$$0.625 \qquad \frac{625}{1,000}$$

thousandths place

Fractions to Decimals

In some situations, decimals are used more commonly than fractions: for example, money situations. At other times, fractions are the more usual form: for example, cooking measurements. You may want to change a fraction to a decimal.

Carpenters make some precise measurements—sometimes in eighths and sixteenths of an inch. It may be helpful to express a fraction as a decimal to compute with a calculator. How do you write $\frac{1}{16}$ as a decimal?

1. Remember that the fraction bar means *divide*.

   $\frac{1}{16}$ is $1 \div 16$

2. Divide the numerator by the denominator.

   $$\frac{1}{16} = \mathbf{0.0625}$$

$$
\begin{array}{r}
0.0625 \\
16\overline{)1.0000} \\
-96 \\
\hline
40 \\
-32 \\
\hline
80 \\
-80 \\
\hline
0
\end{array}
$$

It is helpful to know some common fraction and decimal equivalents.

$\frac{1}{2} = 0.5$	$\frac{1}{4} = 0.25$	$\frac{1}{8} = 0.125$
	$\frac{3}{4} = 0.75$	$\frac{3}{8} = 0.375$
		$\frac{5}{8} = 0.625$
		$\frac{7}{8} = 0.875$

Fraction and Ratio Review Practice 3

A. Write each decimal as a fraction in lowest terms.

1. 0.54

4. 0.1

7. 0.136

2. 0.65

5. 0.08

8. 0.425

3. 0.78

6. 0.392

9. 0.98

B. Write each fraction as a decimal. Round to the thousandths place when necessary.

10. $\frac{3}{20}$

13. $\frac{5}{12}$

16. $\frac{9}{50}$

11. $\frac{9}{10}$

14. $\frac{8}{15}$

17. $\frac{1}{40}$

12. $\frac{3}{5}$

15. $\frac{1}{3}$

18. $\frac{4}{9}$

C. Solve each problem. Then choose the correct answer.

19. Suppose you write the following amount on a check.

Ten and twenty hundredths

How is this amount written in dollars and cents?

(1) $10.002
(2) $10.02
(3) $10.20
(4) $10.25
(5) $20.10

20. Jess wants to write $5\frac{6}{25}$ as a decimal. Which decimal represents $5\frac{6}{25}$?

(1) 5.24
(2) 5.25
(3) 5.265
(4) 5.625
(5) 6.24

21. What is true about the amount of peppers shown on this cash register receipt?

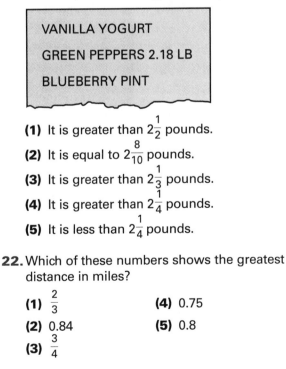

VANILLA YOGURT

GREEN PEPPERS 2.18 LB

BLUEBERRY PINT

(1) It is greater than $2\frac{1}{2}$ pounds.
(2) It is equal to $2\frac{8}{10}$ pounds.
(3) It is greater than $2\frac{1}{3}$ pounds.
(4) It is greater than $2\frac{1}{4}$ pounds.
(5) It is less than $2\frac{1}{4}$ pounds.

22. Which of these numbers shows the greatest distance in miles?

(1) $\frac{2}{3}$

(4) 0.75

(2) 0.84

(5) 0.8

(3) $\frac{3}{4}$

Answers and explanations start on page 85.

Like Fractions

To add fractions, you need to make sure they are like fractions. That means the fractions must have a common denominator.

The following fractions are grouped together to show like fractions.

$$\frac{1}{8}, \frac{3}{8}, \frac{5}{8} \qquad \frac{1}{10}, \frac{3}{10}, \frac{7}{10}, \frac{9}{10}$$

Kevin spent $\frac{1}{4}$ hour preparing the ingredients for a meal and another $\frac{3}{4}$ hour cooking the meal. What was the total time he spent preparing and cooking the meal?

$$\frac{1}{4} + \frac{3}{4} = ?$$

1. Add the numerators.　　　　　　　　　　　　$1 + 3 = 4$

2. Write the sum of the numerators　　　　　$\frac{1}{4} + \frac{3}{4} = \frac{4}{4}$
over the common denominator.

3. Reduce the answer to lowest terms.　　　　$\frac{4}{4} = 1$

Kevin spent **1 hour** preparing and cooking the meal.

Unlike Fractions

You can also add unlike fractions as long as you express them with a common denominator.

A recipe for seafood gumbo calls for $\frac{3}{4}$ pound shrimp, $\frac{2}{3}$ pound scallops, and $\frac{1}{2}$ pound crabmeat. How many pounds of seafood would you need altogether?

$$\frac{3}{4} + \frac{2}{3} + \frac{1}{2} = ?$$

1. Use the multiples of the greatest number to find a common denominator. Change all of the fractions to like fractions.　　　$\frac{3}{4} \quad \frac{3 \times 3}{4 \times 3} = \frac{9}{12}$

$\qquad\qquad\qquad\qquad\qquad\qquad\qquad\qquad\quad \frac{2}{3} \quad \frac{2 \times 4}{3 \times 4} = \frac{8}{12}$

Multiples of 4: 4, 8, 12, 16　　　$\frac{1}{2} \quad \frac{1 \times 6}{2 \times 6} = \frac{6}{12}$

12 is also a multiple of 2 and 3.

2. Add the like fractions.　　　　$\frac{9}{12} + \frac{8}{12} + \frac{6}{12} = \frac{23}{12}$

3. Reduce the answer to lowest terms.　　$\frac{23}{12} = 1\frac{11}{12}$

The recipe calls for $1\frac{11}{12}$ **pounds** of seafood.

Fraction and Ratio Review Practice 4

A. Add. Reduce answers to lowest terms.

1. $\dfrac{1}{5}$
    $+\dfrac{3}{5}$

2. $\dfrac{2}{3}$
    $+\dfrac{1}{6}$

3. $\dfrac{3}{10}$
    $+\dfrac{2}{5}$

4. $\dfrac{2}{9}$
    $+\dfrac{4}{9}$

5. $\dfrac{1}{2}$
    $+\dfrac{5}{12}$

6. $\dfrac{1}{3}$
    $+\dfrac{2}{15}$

7. $\dfrac{1}{10}$
    $+\dfrac{7}{10}$

8. $\dfrac{3}{16}$
    $+\dfrac{1}{8}$

B. Add. Reduce answers to lowest terms. Change improper fractions to whole or mixed numbers.

9. $\dfrac{3}{4} + \dfrac{3}{8} =$

10. $\dfrac{1}{3} + \dfrac{5}{6} =$

11. $\dfrac{7}{8} + \dfrac{1}{4} + \dfrac{1}{2} =$

12. $\dfrac{2}{5} + \dfrac{3}{5} + \dfrac{4}{5} =$

13. $\dfrac{5}{6} + \dfrac{3}{8} =$

14. $\dfrac{7}{12} + \dfrac{7}{12} =$

C. Solve each problem. Then choose the correct answer.

15. Freda mixed $\dfrac{3}{4}$ cup of peanuts with $\dfrac{3}{8}$ cup of cashews and $\dfrac{2}{3}$ cup of dried fruit. How many cups of snack mix did Freda make in all?

    (1) $\dfrac{8}{15}$

    (2) $\dfrac{17}{24}$

    (3) $1\dfrac{19}{24}$

    (4) $1\dfrac{7}{8}$

    (5) $2\dfrac{19}{24}$

16. Thomas runs for $\dfrac{1}{2}$ mile and then walks for $\dfrac{3}{10}$ mile. If he does this 3 times, how many miles has he traveled?

    (1) $2\dfrac{1}{2}$

    (2) $2\dfrac{2}{5}$

    (3) $1\dfrac{3}{5}$

    (4) $1\dfrac{1}{2}$

    (5) $\dfrac{4}{5}$

17. Taylor has a busy accounting business. The graph below shows how Taylor divided her day between her projects. What part of her day was spent working on the Atkinson and Chester projects?

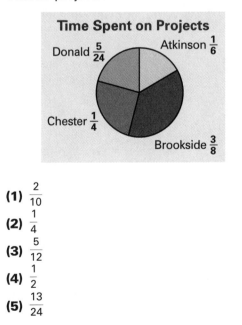

Time Spent on Projects

Donald $\dfrac{5}{24}$ — Atkinson $\dfrac{1}{6}$

Chester $\dfrac{1}{4}$ — Brookside $\dfrac{3}{8}$

    (1) $\dfrac{2}{10}$

    (2) $\dfrac{1}{4}$

    (3) $\dfrac{5}{12}$

    (4) $\dfrac{1}{2}$

    (5) $\dfrac{13}{24}$

Answers and explanations start on page 85.

Like Fractions

As with addition, you can subtract like fractions by simply subtracting the numerators.

Residents of Centerville pay their property taxes quarterly. A quarter of anything is $\frac{1}{4}$ of the whole. After the first quarterly payment, how much of the bill is left to pay?

The whole bill is 1, or $\frac{4}{4}$. $\qquad \frac{4}{4} - \frac{1}{4} = ?$

1. Subtract the numerators. $\qquad\qquad\qquad\qquad 4 - 1 = 3$

2. Write the difference of the numerators over the common denominator. The answer is already in lowest terms. $\qquad \frac{4}{4} - \frac{1}{4} = \frac{3}{4}$

After the first quarterly payment, there is $\frac{3}{4}$ of the bill left to pay.

Unlike Fractions

To subtract unlike fractions, change to a common denominator.

George spends about $\frac{1}{4}$ of his weekly paycheck on rent and $\frac{1}{10}$ on food. How much more of George's paycheck is spent on rent than on food?

1. Find a common denominator and change to like fractions.

$$\frac{1}{4} \quad \frac{1 \times 5}{4 \times 5} = \frac{5}{20}$$

$$\frac{1}{10} \quad \frac{1 \times 2}{10 \times 2} = \frac{2}{20}$$

2. Subtract the numerators of the like fractions. Reduce the answer if necessary.

$$\frac{5}{20} - \frac{2}{20} = \frac{3}{20}$$

George spends $\frac{3}{20}$ more of his paycheck on rent than on food.

Some situations call for subtracting mixed numbers. There are times when a mixed number must be regrouped in order to subtract.

$$5\frac{1}{6} - 2\frac{5}{12} = ?$$

1. Express the numbers as like fractions.

$$5\frac{1}{6} = 5\frac{2}{12}$$

$$5\frac{2}{12} - 2\frac{5}{12} = ?$$

2. Since $\frac{2}{12}$ is less than $\frac{5}{12}$, regroup 1 from the whole number and add it to the fraction.

$$5\frac{2}{12} = 4 + \frac{12}{12} + \frac{2}{12} = 4\frac{14}{12}$$

3. Subtract the mixed numbers and express the answer in lowest terms.

$$4\frac{14}{12} - 2\frac{5}{12} = 2\frac{9}{12} = \mathbf{2\frac{3}{4}}$$

Fraction and Ratio Review Practice 5

A. Subtract. Reduce answers to lowest terms.

1.
$$\begin{array}{r} \frac{7}{8} \\ -\frac{5}{8} \\ \hline \end{array}$$

3.
$$\begin{array}{r} \frac{5}{6} \\ -\frac{2}{3} \\ \hline \end{array}$$

5.
$$\begin{array}{r} \frac{3}{4} \\ -\frac{3}{8} \\ \hline \end{array}$$

7.
$$\begin{array}{r} \frac{11}{12} \\ -\frac{7}{12} \\ \hline \end{array}$$

2.
$$\begin{array}{r} \frac{9}{10} \\ -\frac{3}{5} \\ \hline \end{array}$$

4.
$$\begin{array}{r} \frac{7}{10} \\ -\frac{3}{10} \\ \hline \end{array}$$

6.
$$\begin{array}{r} \frac{11}{15} \\ -\frac{2}{5} \\ \hline \end{array}$$

8.
$$\begin{array}{r} \frac{13}{16} \\ -\frac{1}{8} \\ \hline \end{array}$$

B. Subtract. Regroup the whole number when necessary, and reduce answers to lowest terms.

9.
$$\begin{array}{r} 10\frac{3}{8} \\ -4\frac{5}{8} \\ \hline \end{array}$$

10.
$$\begin{array}{r} 12\frac{1}{4} \\ -9\frac{5}{6} \\ \hline \end{array}$$

11.
$$\begin{array}{r} 4\frac{7}{12} \\ -\frac{3}{8} \\ \hline \end{array}$$

12.
$$\begin{array}{r} 8\frac{2}{5} \\ -3\frac{9}{10} \\ \hline \end{array}$$

C. Solve each problem. Then choose the correct answer.

13. Charles has a pipe that is $8\frac{3}{4}$ feet long. He needs to install a piece of pipe $6\frac{1}{6}$ feet long. How many feet of pipe will Charles cut off?

(1) $14\frac{11}{12}$

(2) $3\frac{7}{12}$

(3) $3\frac{1}{12}$

(4) $2\frac{7}{12}$

(5) $2\frac{1}{6}$

14. It takes Sheila $\frac{1}{4}$ hour to get to work. Mai's ride to work takes $\frac{5}{12}$ hour. Whose ride is longer, and by how much?

(1) Mai's ride is $\frac{1}{6}$ hour longer.

(2) Mai's ride is $\frac{1}{12}$ hour longer.

(3) Sheila's ride is $\frac{1}{6}$ hour longer.

(4) Sheila's ride is $\frac{1}{4}$ hour longer.

(5) Both rides are the same length.

15. Keisha is making salad dressing. She empties a bottle of oil into a measuring cup and measures $\frac{1}{2}$ cup oil. In cups, how much more oil does she need to make the dressing?

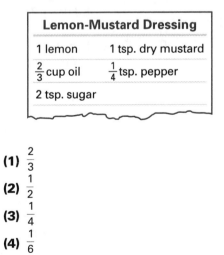

Lemon-Mustard Dressing	
1 lemon	1 tsp. dry mustard
$\frac{2}{3}$ cup oil	$\frac{1}{4}$ tsp. pepper
2 tsp. sugar	

(1) $\frac{2}{3}$

(2) $\frac{1}{2}$

(3) $\frac{1}{4}$

(4) $\frac{1}{6}$

(5) $\frac{1}{8}$

Answers and explanations start on page 86.

Proper Fractions

You can multiply fractions by fractions or fractions by whole numbers.

Angela made a birthday cake, and there was $\frac{3}{4}$ left. She and her family then ate $\frac{2}{3}$ of what was left. How much of the cake did they eat?

$\frac{2}{3}$ of $\frac{3}{4}$ = ?

1. Multiply the numerators. Then multiply the denominators.

$$\frac{2}{3} \times \frac{3}{4} = \frac{6}{12}$$

2. Reduce to lowest terms.

$$\frac{6}{12} = \frac{6 \div 6}{12 \div 6} = \frac{1}{2}$$

Find $\frac{3}{8}$ of 24. (Think: $\frac{3}{8} \times 24$)

Write the whole number as a fraction with a denominator of 1, and multiply. Reduce to lowest terms.

$$\frac{3}{8} \times \frac{24}{1} = \frac{72}{8} = \frac{9}{1} = 9$$

Mixed Numbers

To multiply with mixed numbers, change the mixed number to an improper fraction before multiplying.

Ed put $12\frac{7}{10}$ gallons of gas in his car. He used $\frac{1}{4}$ of this amount driving to the beach. How many gallons of gas did Ed use?

1. Express the mixed number as an improper fraction.

$$12\frac{7}{10} = \frac{12 \times 10 + 7}{10} = \frac{127}{10}$$

2. Multiply the fractions.

$$\frac{1}{4} \times \frac{127}{10} = \frac{127}{40}$$

3. Write the answer as a mixed number.

$$\frac{127}{40} = 3\frac{7}{40}$$

Ed used **$3\frac{7}{40}$ gallons of gas.**

Canceling

Sometimes when multiplying fractions, you can cancel to simplify the problem before multiplying.

Multiply $3\frac{3}{4}$ by $\frac{2}{5}$.

1. Change the mixed number to an improper fraction.

$$3\frac{3}{4} = \frac{15}{4}$$

2. Factor the numerator and denominator by the same number. Factor out 5 from 15 and 5. Factor out 2 from 4 and 2.

$$\frac{\overset{3}{\cancel{15}}}{\underset{2}{\cancel{4}}} \times \frac{\overset{1}{\cancel{2}}}{\underset{1}{\cancel{5}}}$$

3. Multiply the numerators, and multiply the denominators.

$$\frac{3}{2} \times \frac{1}{1} = \frac{3}{2}$$

4. Simplify the answer.

$$\frac{3}{2} = 1\frac{1}{2}$$

Fraction and Ratio Review Practice 6

A. Multiply. Use canceling when possible. Reduce answers to lowest terms.

1. $\dfrac{3}{8} \times \dfrac{3}{5}$

2. $\dfrac{2}{3} \times \dfrac{4}{9}$

3. $\dfrac{3}{4}$ of 28

4. $\dfrac{1}{5} \times \dfrac{3}{8}$

5. $\dfrac{9}{10} \times \dfrac{5}{12}$

6. $\dfrac{1}{4} \times \dfrac{4}{5}$

7. $\dfrac{1}{3}$ of 120

8. $\dfrac{5}{8} \times \dfrac{2}{9}$

9. $\dfrac{1}{10} \times \dfrac{3}{5}$

B. Multiply. Use canceling when possible. Reduce answers to lowest terms.

10. $\dfrac{4}{5} \times 3\dfrac{3}{10}$

11. $5\dfrac{1}{5} \times 2\dfrac{7}{8}$

12. $\dfrac{7}{12} \times 4\dfrac{1}{3}$

13. $\dfrac{1}{2} \times 8\dfrac{1}{8}$

14. $1\dfrac{1}{4} \times 9\dfrac{1}{3}$

15. $\dfrac{1}{3}$ of $12\dfrac{2}{3}$

C. Solve each problem. Then choose the correct answer.

16. The diagram below shows the measurements of a kitchen floor. The area, in square feet, equals the length multiplied by the width. A tile layer has completed tiling $\dfrac{3}{4}$ of the floor. How many square feet have been tiled?

(1) 50
(2) 100
(3) 150
(4) 180
(5) 200

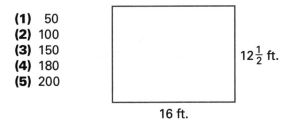

16 ft.

12½ ft.

17. Joe cuts $\dfrac{1}{2}$ of a cake into 8 pieces. Each piece is what fraction of the original cake?

(1) $\dfrac{1}{2}$

(2) $\dfrac{1}{4}$

(3) $\dfrac{1}{8}$

(4) $\dfrac{1}{10}$

(5) $\dfrac{1}{16}$

18. A recipe calls for $2\dfrac{1}{4}$ cups of flour. Donald is making $\dfrac{1}{3}$ of the recipe. How many cups of flour will Donald use?

(1) $\dfrac{2}{3}$

(2) $\dfrac{3}{4}$

(3) $1\dfrac{1}{4}$

(4) $1\dfrac{3}{4}$

(5) $2\dfrac{7}{12}$

19. A butcher is packaging ground beef. One package is made using $\dfrac{1}{4}$ of the meat in the bin. How many pounds of ground beef are in this package?

(1) $2\dfrac{1}{8}$

(2) $3\dfrac{1}{8}$

(3) $3\dfrac{1}{4}$

(4) $4\dfrac{1}{8}$

(5) $8\dfrac{1}{2}$

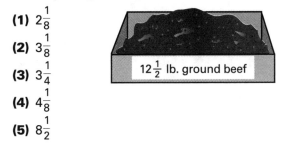

12½ lb. ground beef

Answers and explanations start on page 86.

Proper Fractions

To make sense out of a problem with division of fractions, think about the relationship between multiplication and division.

$$\frac{3}{4} \div \frac{1}{8} = ?$$

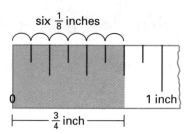

six $\frac{1}{8}$ inches

0   1 inch

$\frac{3}{4}$ inch

Another way to look at this problem is to say "How many $\frac{1}{8}$s are there in $\frac{3}{4}$?" Look at the ruler above. There are six $\frac{1}{8}$s in $\frac{3}{4}$.

Since multiplication and division are opposite operations, you can use inverse operations when dividing fractions.

When dividing with fractions, first change the $\div$ sign to a $\times$ sign. Next, invert the fraction that follows the $\div$ sign. This inverted fraction is called the reciprocal. Then multiply and reduce.

$$\frac{3}{4} \div \frac{1}{8} = ?$$

1. Write a multiplication problem with the reciprocal of the divisor.

$$\frac{3}{4} \div \frac{1}{8} = \frac{3}{4} \times \frac{8}{1}$$

2. Multiply, and reduce to lowest terms.

$$\frac{3}{4} \times \frac{8}{1} = \frac{24}{4} = 6$$

$\frac{3}{4} \div \frac{1}{8} = $ **6**, which is the same answer shown in the drawing above.

Mixed Numbers

You can use this procedure to divide whole numbers or mixed numbers by fractions.

An art teacher is cutting $\frac{1}{2}$-inch strips from a sheet of paper $8\frac{1}{2}$ inches wide. How many strips can she cut from the sheet of paper?

1. Express the mixed number as an improper fraction.

$$8\frac{1}{2} = \frac{17}{2}$$

2. Write a division problem. Use the reciprocal of the divisor to write a multiplication problem.

$$\frac{17}{2} \div \frac{1}{2} = \frac{17}{2} \times \frac{2}{1}$$

3. Multiply and reduce to lowest terms.

$$\frac{17}{\overset{}{\underset{1}{2}}} \times \frac{\overset{1}{2}}{1} = \frac{17}{1} = 17$$

The teacher can cut **17 half-inch strips** from the sheet of paper.

Fraction and Ratio Review Practice 7

A. Divide. Reduce answers to lowest terms.

1. $\dfrac{2}{3} \div \dfrac{1}{6} =$

2. $\dfrac{5}{8} \div \dfrac{3}{4} =$

3. $\dfrac{7}{12} \div \dfrac{2}{3} =$

4. $\dfrac{4}{5} \div \dfrac{3}{10} =$

5. $\dfrac{2}{9} \div \dfrac{1}{3} =$

6. $\dfrac{7}{8} \div \dfrac{1}{4} =$

7. $\dfrac{11}{12} \div \dfrac{5}{6} =$

8. $\dfrac{1}{2} \div \dfrac{1}{10} =$

9. $\dfrac{3}{5} \div \dfrac{9}{10} =$

B. Divide. Reduce answers to lowest terms.

10. $15 \div \dfrac{5}{8} =$

11. $3\dfrac{3}{8} \div \dfrac{3}{4} =$

12. $8\dfrac{7}{10} \div 3 =$

13. $24 \div 4\dfrac{1}{6} =$

14. $9\dfrac{1}{4} \div 1\dfrac{7}{8} =$

15. $12 \div 1\dfrac{1}{8} =$

C. Solve each problem. Then choose the correct answer.

16. Dion is stacking books in this box. If each book has the same width, how many books will fit in one stack?

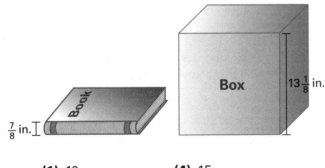

(1) 10

(2) $11\dfrac{31}{64}$

(3) $14\dfrac{6}{7}$

(4) 15

(5) 16

17. Wes works at The Game Gallery. He is making a display with decks of cards. Each deck is $2\dfrac{5}{8}$ inches wide. The shelf is $47\dfrac{1}{4}$ inches wide. How many decks will fit on the shelf side by side?

(1) $124\dfrac{1}{32}$

(2) $49\dfrac{7}{8}$

(3) $44\dfrac{1}{2}$

(4) 20

(5) 18

18. How many $\dfrac{1}{4}$-inch pencils will fit in a package $1\dfrac{1}{2}$ inches wide?

(1) 10

(2) 8

(3) 6

(4) 5

(5) 4

19. A sandwich shop has 24 pounds of meat. How many 12-inch sandwiches can the shop make?

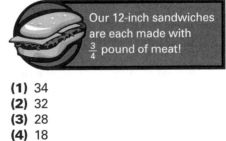

Our 12-inch sandwiches are each made with $\dfrac{3}{4}$ pound of meat!

(1) 34

(2) 32

(3) 28

(4) 18

(5) 12

Answers and explanations start on page 86.

Write Ratios

One way to compare two numbers is by using a ratio.

Look at the directions listed on the can. The ratio of water to concentrate is **3 to 1.**

This ratio can also be written as **3:1** or $\frac{3}{1}$.

Notice that the words in the ratio are *water* to *concentrate*. The numbers in the ratio must match the order of the words. If you wrote the ratio *1 to 3*, it would show the comparison of *concentrate to water*.

APPLE JUICE

Mix contents with 3 cans of water.

Reduce Ratios

Ratios are like fractions in many ways. Like a fraction, a ratio can be simplified by dividing both numbers by the same number.

In a preschool class, there are 3 teachers and 21 students. What is the ratio of students to teachers in lowest terms?

1. Write a ratio.

21 to 3 or $\frac{21}{3}$

2. Simplify the ratio to lowest terms. Divide both numbers by the same number.

$\frac{21 \div 3}{3 \div 3} = \frac{7}{1}$

3. A ratio must have two terms, so keep the number 1 when you write the simplified ratio.

$\frac{7}{1}$ or **7 to 1** or **7:1**

Although ratios can be simplified as fractions can, they should not be expressed as whole number or mixed numbers. Remember that a ratio is a comparison of two numbers.

Compute to Find Ratio Terms

Some ratio problems do not give all of the necessary numbers. You may have to do some type of calculation before you can write a ratio.

Of the 84 customers, only 24 were men. What is the ratio of women to men customers?

1. Find the number of women customers. Subtract the number of men from the total number of customers.

84 − 24 = 60
60 women

2. Write a ratio in the correct order.

$\frac{60 \text{ women}}{24 \text{ men}}$

3. Simplify the ratio when necessary.

$\frac{60 \div 12}{24 \div 12} = \frac{5}{2}$

The ratio of women customers to men customers is **5 to 2.**

Fraction and Ratio Review Practice 8

A. Write each ratio as a fraction in lowest terms.

1. 64 paperback books to 32 hardcover books

2. 30 vans to 100 cars

3. $150 to $100

4. 8 pounds to 6 pounds

5. 14 inches to 12 inches

6. 64 ounces of gasoline to 2 ounces of oil

7. 16 wins to 4 losses

8. 500 cans to 300 bottles

9. 15 hits to 5 strikeouts

10. 40 hours to 32 hours

B. Find each ratio.

11. The Horizon Group has 51 employees of which 6 are under the age of 20. What is the ratio of employees under 20 to employees 20 and over?

12. A flower arrangement has a total of 30 flowers. There are 18 daffodils, and the rest are tulips. What is the ratio of tulips to total flowers?

13. In a bag of fruit, there are 8 apples and 10 oranges. What is the ratio of apples to total pieces of fruit?

14. A box of 24 crayons contains 20 different colors. The rest are shades of blue. What is the ratio of blue crayons to total crayons?

C. Solve each problem. Then choose the correct answer.

Questions 15 and 16 refer to the information below.

15. The information below is from a nutritional label for dried fruit. What is the ratio of calories to serving size?

Dried Fruit	
Serving Size 30 g	
Calories	100
Calories from fat	15
Carbohydrates 22 g	
Protein 1 g	

(1) 100 calories to 3 grams fruit
(2) 15 calories to 3 grams fruit
(3) 10 calories to 3 grams fruit
(4) 10 calories to 30 grams fruit
(5) 1 calorie to 15 grams fruit

16. What is the ratio of carbohydrates to serving size of dried fruit?

(1) $\frac{11}{50}$ (4) $\frac{22}{15}$

(2) $\frac{11}{15}$ (5) $\frac{22}{1}$

(3) $\frac{15}{11}$

17. In a lacrosse game, the Warriors scored 12 goals and the Nets scored 3 goals. Which statement is true about the game?

(1) The Warriors outscored the Nets 3 to 1.
(2) The Nets outscored the Warriors 2 to 1.
(3) The Nets outscored the Warriors 3 to 1.
(4) The Warriors outscored the Nets 4 to 1.
(5) The Nets outscored the Warriors 4 to 1.

Answers and explanations start on page 87.

Cross Products

An equation that shows two equal ratios is called a proportion. As with equivalent fractions, cross products in a proportion are equal.

The scale on a map states that 1 inch = 25 miles. A measurement of 4 inches would represent 100 miles.

$$\frac{\text{inches}}{\text{miles}} \quad \frac{1}{25} \diagup\!\!\!\!\diagdown \frac{4}{100}$$

$$1 \times 100 = 25 \times 4$$
$$100 = 100$$

|——————————————————|
1 inch = 25 miles

Remember to write the parts of both ratios in the same order.

Solve for the Missing Term

You can use cross products to solve problems that use proportions. The cross products will help you find the missing number in a proportion.

Smart-Buy Supermarket sells 5 pounds of potatoes for $1.75. At this rate, how much would you pay for 8 pounds of potatoes?

POTATOES
5 pounds for $1.75

1. Write two ratios to compare pounds to price. Use a variable for the unknown.

$$\frac{\text{pounds}}{\text{price}} = \frac{5}{\$1.75} = \frac{8}{x}$$

2. Find the cross product.

$$\$1.75 \times 8 = \$14$$

3. Divide by the remaining known number.

$$\$14 \div 5 = \$2.80$$

Eight pounds of potatoes would cost **$2.80** at the supermarket.

Find the Rate

Proportions can be used to find rates. A rate is a comparison of two different kinds of units. Many rates use the word *per* to compare units. A unit rate is a ratio with a denominator of 1.

The label on a package of frozen muffins recommends the following microwave reheating time.

4 muffins	60 seconds

Sophia wants to reheat only 1 muffin. Based on the package directions, how many seconds of reheating are recommended per muffin?

1. Write two ratios to compare seconds to muffins.

$$\frac{\text{seconds}}{\text{muffin}} = \frac{60}{4} = \frac{x}{1}$$

2. Find the cross product.

$$60 \times 1 = 60$$

3. Divide by the remaining known number.

$$60 \div 4 = 15$$

The directions recommend reheating for
15 seconds per muffin.

Fraction and Ratio Review Practice 9

A. Solve for the missing term.

1. $\dfrac{30}{40} = \dfrac{x}{100}$

2. $\dfrac{7}{x} = \dfrac{56}{64}$

3. $\dfrac{3}{2} = \dfrac{24}{x}$

4. $\dfrac{12}{x} = \dfrac{32}{40}$

5. $\dfrac{10}{7} = \dfrac{x}{49}$

6. $\dfrac{x}{19} = \dfrac{60}{76}$

7. $\dfrac{8}{21} = \dfrac{40}{x}$

8. $\dfrac{4}{x} = \dfrac{48}{36}$

9. $\dfrac{11}{40} = \dfrac{88}{x}$

10. $\dfrac{x}{35} = \dfrac{9}{45}$

11. $\dfrac{3}{5} = \dfrac{x}{110}$

12. $\dfrac{18}{4} = \dfrac{36}{x}$

B. Find each unit rate.

13. 4 miles in 24 minutes

14. 120 miles on 6 gallons

15. $1,125 in 5 days

16. $2.56 for 32 ounces

17. 280 people for 14 groups

18. $33.75 for 5 tickets

C. Solve each problem. Then choose the correct answer.

19. An architect is making a model of a building he is designing. He will use a scale of $\frac{1}{2}$ inch = 1 foot. The diagram shows the measurements of the door for this building. What will be the height of the door on the model, in inches?

    (1) 20
    (2) 15
    (3) 10
    (4) 5
    (5) 4

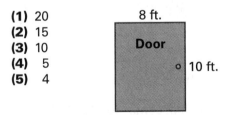

8 ft.

Door

○ 10 ft.

20. One cup of pancake mix is needed for 4 servings. How many cups of mix would you use to make 10 servings?

    (1) $1\frac{1}{2}$
    (2) $1\frac{3}{4}$
    (3) 2
    (4) $2\frac{1}{2}$
    (5) $2\frac{3}{4}$

21. A private school promises to maintain a ratio of 6 students per teacher. At that rate, how many teachers are needed for a total of 282 students?

    (1) 45
    (2) 47
    (3) 48
    (4) 50
    (5) 52

Answers and explanations start on page 87.

Parts of a Percent Problem

A percent is another way to show part of a whole. Percent means per 100 parts. Percent problems consist of three elements: the base, the rate, and the part.

The base is the original amount, or 16 ounces. The other numbers are compared to the base. The part is how much more shampoo, or 4 ounces. It is a part of the base. The rate is the percent (25%), which defines the relationship between the part and the base.

base   part

$16 \times 25\% = 4$

     rate

$25\% = \dfrac{25}{100} = 0.25$

$16 \times 0.25 = 4$

Find the Part

Percent problems ask for a missing element. You can use the percent formula to find a missing element: base × rate = part.

Helen sells a home theater system with a price of $689. What is the discount?

The discount is the part, or the amount taken off the price.

November Special

20% off all home theater systems

1. Write the equation.   base × rate = part

2. Substitute values into the equation. $689 × 20% = part

3. Change the percent to a decimal and multiply. $689 × 0.20 = $137.80

The discount on the home theater system is **$137.80**.

Sometimes you are asked to find the discounted price. To find the discounted price, subtract the discount from the original price.

$689.00 − $137.80 = **$551.20**

Other problems require finding the part and then adding.

Lee gives the waiter a 15% tip for a bill that comes to $75.20. What is the total amount Lee pays, including tip?

tip: 15% × $75.20 = 0.15 × $75.20 = $11.28

Add the tip to the cost of the meal: $75.20 + $11.28 = **$86.48**.

Percent Problems Practice 1

A. Identify the underlined number as *part*, *base*, or *rate*.

1. 10% of <u>50</u> = 5

2. 15% of 45 = <u>6.75</u>

3. <u>58%</u> of 2,000 = 1,160

4. 14% of 256 = <u>35.84</u>

5. <u>60%</u> of 84 = 50.4

6. 42% of <u>100</u> = 42

7. 75% of <u>1,200</u> = 900

8. 50% of <u>400</u> = 200

9. 65% of 2,400 = <u>1,560</u>

B. Solve as directed.

10. Find 50% of 628.

11. What is 3% of 4,200?

12. What is 30% of 90?

13. Find 20% of 350.

14. What is 33% of 6,000?

15. Find 25% of 250.

16. What is 18% of 50?

17. Find 22% of 400.

C. Solve each problem. Then choose the correct answer.

18. This table shows the results of a town election. If there were 5,000 voters, how many votes did candidate Romano receive?

Candidate	Percent of Votes
Miller	31%
Romano	56%
Gray	13%

   (1)   560
   (2)   650
   (3) 1,550
   (4) 2,800
   (5) 2,850

19. How many more votes did Romano receive than Gray?

   (1)   43
   (2)   900
   (3) 1,250
   (4) 2,150
   (5) 2,175

20. What is the sale price for this item?

Regular Price $48.00
SALE TODAY 15% OFF

   (1) $42.80
   (2) $40.80
   (3) $40.00
   (4) $33.00
   (5) $7.20

21. Each week Deb puts 8% of her take-home pay in a retirement account. If her take-home pay is $416, how much does she put in her retirement account each week?

   (1) $424.00
   (2) $408.00
   (3) $33.28
   (4) $33.24
   (5) $24.00

Answers and explanations start on page 87.

Identify What to
Solve For

You have learned the three elements of a percent problem. To solve a percent problem, you must identify the elements you already know and then solve for the missing element.

In a free-throw contest, Carlos took 50 shots and made 45 baskets. What percent of the shots were baskets?

Total shots = 50   base = 50
The part that were baskets = 45   part = 45
What is the percent?   rate = ?

In this problem, the missing element is the rate. The question asks for a percent. This gives the clue that you need to find the rate.

Find the Rate

When solving for the rate, remember that the rate is the percent. If *base* × *rate* = *part*, then *rate* = *part* ÷ *base*. In the problem above, rate = 45 ÷ 50 = 0.9 = **90%.**

The chart shows the kinds and numbers of automobiles sold at Ace's Auto Sales during one month. What percent of total sales are trucks?

Ace's Auto Sales	
Cars	55
Vans	17
Trucks	48
Total	120

You know the base (total sales): 120.
You know the part (truck sales): 48.
Find the rate: rate = part ÷ base.
Express as a percent.

$48 \div 120 = 0.4$

$0.4 = \frac{40}{100} = 40\%$

Trucks were **40% of total sales.**

In many percent problems, you will need to do some calculation before you can use the formula.

A company has 64 full-time employees and 16 part-time employees. What percent of the company's employees work part-time?

The base is the total number of employees. First, add to find the total number of employees.
    64 full-time + 16 part-time = 80
The part is the number of part-time employees, or 16.

Find the rate: rate = part ÷ base
                 rate = 16 ÷ 80 = 0.2 = 20%

20% of the employees work part-time.

Percent Problems Practice 2

A. Solve.

1. $15 is what percent of $250?

2. 440 is what percent of 2,000?

3. What percent of 200 is 30?

4. What percent of 50 is 19?

5. 6 is what percent of 8?

6. What percent of 80 is 48?

7. $20 is what percent of $400?

8. What percent of 12 is 3.6?

B. Find the rate.

9. 18 out of 48 women

10. 9 out of 10 doctors

11. 128 out of 1,600 books

12. 420 out of 1,000 people surveyed

13. 24 payments made out of 60

14. $28 out of a total bill of $80

15. 680 out of 800 members

16. 1 out of 10 drivers

C. Solve each problem. Then choose the correct answer.

17. One day a veterinarian practice treated 33 dogs and 27 cats. What percent of the animals treated were dogs?

   (1) 27%
   (2) 33%
   (3) 45%
   (4) 55%
   (5) 82%

18. On a test with 50 items, there are 4 open-response questions. What percent of the items are open-response questions?

   (1) 4%
   (2) 7%
   (3) 8%
   (4) 80%
   (5) 88%

19. Below is the payment portion of a construction contract. What percent of the total bill is the final payment?

Payment Plan	
Stage	**Amount**
Deposit	$ 6,000
Foundation in	$12,000
Rough Inspection	$24,000
Final	$18,000

   (1) 6%
   (2) 18%
   (3) 20%
   (4) 30%
   (5) 60%

Answers and explanations start on page 88.

Identify What to Solve For

As you know, the first step in solving a percent problem is to identify the elements you know. Then you solve for the element that is missing. Some problems give the rate and part, and you must find the base.

City College states that 24% of its students receive some kind of scholarship. This year 300 students have scholarships. How many students are attending City College this year?

This problem gives the part (300 students with scholarships) and the rate (24%). The missing element is the base, or the total number of students attending the college.

Find the Base

Use the formula to solve for the base. If *base* × *rate* = *part*, then ***base* = *part* ÷ *rate*.** In the problem above, the base is 300. Divide: $300 \div 0.24 = 1{,}250$. This year **1,250 students** are attending City College.

Next month Sharon will receive a salary increase of $1.00 per hour. This is a 7.5% raise to her current hourly wage. How much money does Sharon earn per hour now?

You know the part: $1.00 $1.00 ÷ 7.5% = $1 ÷ 0.075 = $13.333. . .
You know the rate: 7.5%
Find the base:
base = part ÷ rate   Round to the nearest cent. **$13.33**

Percents Greater than 100%

Rates can be greater than 100%. If so, the part is greater than the base.

The Hart family's budget is greater this year. This year's insurance bill is 110% percent of last year's bill. What was last year's insurance bill?

Hart Family Budget		
	Last Year	This Year
Groceries	$5,200	$6,500
Insurance (Auto)	?	$693

part: this year's bill of $693
rate: 110%
Find the base:
base = part ÷ rate

$$\text{base} = \underset{\text{part}}{\$693} \div \underset{\text{rate}}{110\%} =$$
$693 ÷ 1.1 = **$630**
Note that the part is greater than the base.

You can solve for other elements in the percent formula. This year's grocery bill is 125% of last year's bill. Use the formula, *part* ÷ *base* = *rate*: $6,500 ÷ $5,200 = 1.25 = **125%.**

Percent Problems Practice 3

A. Find the base.

1. $6.30 is 18% of what amount?

2. 32% of what number is 96?

3. 70% of what amount is 175 pounds?

4. 1,485 is 45% of what number?

5. $48 is 50% of what amount?

6. 25% of what amount is 15.5 kilograms?

7. 144 is 120% of what number?

8. 68% of what number is 3,400?

B. Solve.

9. $2,650 is what percent of $1,325?

10. Find 130% of 58.

11. 350% of what number is 315?

12. 115% of what amount is $230?

13. 93 is what percent of 62?

14. Find 220% of $2,000.

15. What percent of 400 is 700?

16. 160% of 85 is what number?

C. Solve each problem. Then choose the correct answer.

17. In the most recent town election, 3,344 people voted. This number is 64% of all registered voters in town. How many registered voters are there in all?

    (1)   523
    (2) 2,140
    (3) 3,408
    (4) 5,225
    (5) 21,401

18. In problem 17, the number of voters in this election was 160% of the voters in the last election. Which expression shows the number of voters in the last election?

    (1) 3,344 ÷ 1.6
    (2) 1.6 × 3,344
    (3) 3,344 ÷ 160
    (4) 5,225 ÷ 1.6
    (5) 1.6 × 5,225

19. What is the original price for a gallon of paint?

    (1) $30.00
    (2) $25.00
    (3) $20.00
    (4) $15.00
    (5) $10.00

20. Last month Cam's Caterers made 6,600 meals. This month they made 8,910 meals. This month's meals are what percent of last month's meals?

    (1) 13.5%
    (2) 26%
    (3) 75%
    (4) 135%
    (5) 231%

Answers and explanations start on page 88.

Percent of Increase

In some percent problems, you are asked to find a rate of change. You can solve these problems by finding a percent of increase or decrease.

In the first year it was held, an annual charity event raised $5,200. In the second year, the event raised $6,136. What was the percent of increase from the first year to the second year?

> **10K Walk for Hunger**
>
> April 25 – Grant Park
> For Details Call
> 1-800-FOR-FOOD

1. Find the difference between the original number and the new number.

   $6,136 − $5,200 = $936

   new   original

2. Divide the difference by the original number.

   $936 ÷ $5,200 = 0.18

3. Express as a percent.

   0.18 = **18% increase**

It is important to divide the difference by the original number, that is, the number the increase is being compared to.

Percent of Decrease

In some situations the rate of change is a decrease.

The town of Milton has proposed a tax decrease. A property owner who now pays $2,400 in taxes would pay $2,328. What is the proposed percent of decrease in property taxes?

1. Find the difference between the original number and the new number.

   2,400 − 2,328 = 72

2. Divide the difference by the original number.

   72 ÷ 2,400 = 0.03

3. Express as a percent.

   0.03 = **3% tax cut**

Percent of Increase Greater than 100%

In some cases, the rate is greater than 100%.

When Katrina started driving, the average price for a gallon of gas was $0.50. Now the average price is $1.80 per gallon. What is the percent of increase in gas price?

$1.80 − $0.50 = $1.30 and $1.30 ÷ $0.50 = 2.6 or **260%**

Percent Problems Practice 4

A. Write *increase* or *decrease* to describe each situation.

1. 1,200 people in May and 1,800 people in June

2. change in price from $650 to $480

3. 5,400 attendees last year to 5,800 attendees this year

4. an adjustment from $890 to $875

B. Find the percent of increase or decrease.

5. from 48 to 72

6. from 1,500 to 300

7. from 600 to 300

8. from 2,000 to 3,200

9. from 250 to 170

10. from 1,400 to 3,500

11. from 1,800 to 2,340

12. from 840 to 630

13. from 200 to 640

14. from 350 to 315

15. from 800 to 200

16. from 25 to 26

C. Solve each problem. Then choose the correct answer.

17. Membership at a gym varies from month to month. What is the rate of change of adult membership from August to September?

Monthly Membership Fun & Fitness		
	August	September
Adult	400	460
Youth	120	36

(1) 12.5% increase
(2) 60% increase
(3) 13% increase
(4) 15% decrease
(5) 15% increase

18. In problem 17, what is the rate of change of youth membership from August to September?

(1) 70% decrease
(2) 70% increase
(3) 36% decrease
(4) 78% decrease
(5) 233% decrease

19. A house was on the market for the price shown on the sign. The house did not sell, so the owners then listed the house at $154,000. What is the rate of change?

HOUSE FOR SALE
Asking Price: $160,000

(1) 60% decrease
(2) 37.5% decrease
(3) 3.9% decrease
(4) 3.755% increase
(5) 3.75% decrease

20. Ten years ago school enrollment was 1,850 students. Now it is 3,885 students. What is the rate of change during the 10-year period?

(1) 11% increase
(2) 52.4% decrease
(3) 110% increase
(4) 110% decrease
(5) 210% increase

Answers and explanations start on page 88.

How to Read Tables

One way to organize data is in a table. In a table, the data is displayed in rows and columns. Titles and labels describe the data.

Tide Table				
Day	**A.M. High**	**A.M. Low**	**P.M. High**	**P.M. Low**
1		6:02	12:17	6:11
2	12:28	6:54	1:09	7:05
3	1:22	7:44	1:59	7:59
4	2:14	8:33	2:49	8:53
5	3:06	9:21	3:38	9:47

title → Tide Table
labels → A.M. Low, P.M. Low
row → 2
column

Locate Information

To find information in a table, use the column and row headings to navigate. Follow the appropriate row across and the appropriate column down to the place where the column and row meet.

Martin wants to collect some clams. He plans to go on the second day of the month in the morning. Martin has to go at low tide. At what time in the morning is low tide on this day?

1. Find the row labeled *Day 2*.
2. Find the column labeled A.M. *Low.*
3. Read the time where the column and row meet.

The morning low tide on the second day of the month is at **6:54** A.M.

Interpret Frequency Tables

One specific type of table is a frequency table. It is a way to record how often events occur.

Alicia owns a sporting goods store. One day she tracked sales by recording the number of items sold in each department. How many items were sold from the clothing and shoe departments?

Frequency Table: Sales 3/15	
Department	**Number of Items**
Camping	卌 卌 //
Clothing	卌 卌 卌 卌 卌 卌 ////
Sports	卌 卌 卌 卌 ////
Shoe	卌 卌 卌 //

Find the rows labeled *Clothing* and *Shoe*. Count the tally marks. *Clothing* has 34 tally marks, and *Shoe* has 17 tally marks. Add to find the total: 34 + 17 = 51. There were **51 items sold** from the clothing and shoe departments.

Data Analysis Practice 1

A. Questions 1–4 refer to the table below.

Flowering Bulbs			
Flower Name	Height (in inches)	Color	Season of Bloom
Lily Leek	15	Yellow	May–June
Crocus	5	Blue, Yellow, White, Purple	April
Summer Hyacinth	48	White	July–August
Hardy Amaryllis	24–36	Purple	August

1. If you want a plant with yellow flowers, what are your choices?

2. Which flower blooms the earliest in the year?

3. Cindy wants to plant a tall flower that can go in the back of her garden. What is her best choice?

4. Which flowers will bloom in either July or August?

B. Questions 5–7 refer to the frequency table below.

5. During which time period did Janet receive the fewest orders?

6. How many more orders did Janet receive between 4:01 and 8:00 P.M. than between 8:00 A.M. and 12:00?

7. How many orders did Janet receive in all?

Telephone Orders	Received by Janet 10/21
Hours	Orders Received
8:00 A.M.–12:00 noon	ЖΗ ЖΗ II
12:01 P.M.–4:00 P.M.	ЖΗ ЖΗ
4:01 P.M.–8:00 P.M.	ЖΗ ЖΗ ЖΗ IIII

C. Solve each problem. Then choose the correct answer.

8. What is the time difference between sunrise and sunset on day 3?

Sunrise and Sunset Times		
Day	Rise A.M.	Set P.M.
1	5:17	8:12
2	5:18	8:11
3	5:19	8:10
4	5:20	8:09

(1) 15 hours 9 minutes
(2) 14 hours 56 minutes
(3) 14 hours 51 minutes
(4) 14 hours 41 minutes
(5) 2 hours 51 minutes

9. Employees voted for the place to hold the annual picnic.

Place	Number of Votes
Amusement Park	ЖΗ ЖΗ ЖΗ III
Lake	ЖΗ ЖΗ II
Resort	ЖΗ ЖΗ ЖΗ ЖΗ

What percent of the employees chose a resort?

(1) 20%
(2) 24%
(3) 36%
(4) 40%
(5) 50%

Answers and explanations start on page 89.

Find the Average

To compare the pieces of data in a group, you can find the typical values. The average, or mean, is often used to describe a typical number for a data set. The other numbers in the data set can be compared to the average.

This table shows the high temperatures each day for one week. What is the mean high temperature for the week?

Mon.	Tue.	Wed.	Thu.	Fri.	Sat.	Sun.
70°	70°	66°	65°	69°	67°	69°

1. Add the numbers. $70° + 70° + 66° + 65° + 69° + 67° + 69° = 476°$
2. Divide by the number of items in the set (7). $476° \div 7 = 68°$

The mean high temperature for the week is **68°.**

Find the Median

A second measure used to show a typical value in a data set is the median. The median is the middle value.

Find the median temperature for the week.

1. Arrange the numbers in order. 65°, 66°, 67°, 69°, 69°, 70°, 70°
2. Find the middle number. 3 numbers|middle|3 numbers

Since 69° is the middle number, the median temperature is **69°.**

Some data sets have an even number of values, so there are two middle numbers. When this happens, find the mean of the two middle numbers.

1. Find the two middle numbers. 13, 15, 15, 16, 18, 18, 18, 19
2. Find the mean of 16 and 18. $16 + 18 = 34$, and $34 \div 2 = 17$

The median for this group of numbers is **17.**

Identify the Mode

The mode of a data set is the number that appears most often. In the group of numbers above, 18 is the mode since it occurs most often—three times. The other values appear only once or twice. A set of values can have more than one mode.

What is the mode of the set of temperatures from the table?
70°, 70°, 66°, 65°, 69°, 67°, 69°

This set of data has two modes: **69° and 70°.** Both values occur twice, while the remaining values occur only once.

A data set has no mode if there is no number that occurs more often than any other. The data set 98, 87, 89, 92, 88, 85 has no mode.

Data Analysis Practice 2

A. Find the mean, median, and mode for each group of numbers.

1. 20, 20, 30, 30, 30, 40, 40

2. 524, 528, 504, 510, 530, 524

3. 85, 82, 77, 73, 82, 89, 79

4. $4.10, $4.40, $3.95, $4.50, $3.75, $4.25, $4.40, $4.25

5. 8.1, 7.9, 8.5, 8.0, 7.8, 8.6, 8.5

6. 1,600; 1,500; 1,800; 1,200; 1,500

7. 212, 230, 235, 239, 256, 204, 213, 235

8. 14, 18, 12, 12, 19, 12, 18

B. Find the mean, median, and mode for each data set.

9. prices for an airplane flight: $395, $415, $435, $375, $450, $415, $470, $445

10. ages of members of a band: 28, 31, 33, 30, 36, 34

11. bowling scores: 106, 98, 109, 115, 100, 102, 106, 102, 110, 102

12. neighborhood house values: $182,000; $186,000; $183,000; $172,000; $179,000

C. Solve each problem. Then choose the correct answer.

13. The following are the heights of the starting lineup of a basketball team. What is the median height of these players, in inches?

77 in., 79 in., 82 in., 80 in., 78 in.

(1) 77
(2) 78
(3) 79
(4) 79.5
(5) 80

14. Which of these expressions would you use to find the mean height of the players in question 13?

(1) $(77 + 79 + 82 + 80 + 78) - 5$
(2) $(77 + 79 + 82 + 80 + 78) \div 4$
(3) $77 + 79 + 82 + 80 + 78$
(4) $(77 + 79 + 82 + 80 + 78) \times 5$
(5) $(77 + 79 + 82 + 80 + 78) \div 5$

15. The books below are reading assignments for an English class. What is the mean number of pages in this group of books?

(1) 132
(2) 158.4
(3) 160
(4) 164
(5) 184

Answers and explanations start on page 89.

How to Read Bar Graphs

Bar graphs are used to compare different data about similar topics. The bars visually represent the numbers. This graph shows grant money awarded for research by a wildlife organization.

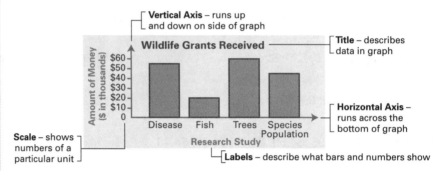

How much grant money was awarded for studying trees and diseases?

Find the bar for trees. Look at the end of the bar. Follow it to the scale. It aligns with $60, which means $60,000.

Do the same with the bar for disease. It is about halfway between $50 and $60, which is $55. This stands for $55,000.

Add the numbers to find the total: $60,000 + $55,000 = **$115,000.**

Explore Double-Bar Graphs

A double-bar graph is used to compare two sets of data. Notice that this graph has a key, which gives extra information that is necessary to read the graph. The key shows what the different-color bars represent.

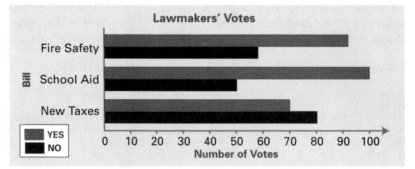

How many more lawmakers voted *Yes* than *No* for the fire safety bill?

Look at the key. The blue bar stands for a *Yes* vote, and the black bar stands for a *No* vote.

Follow down from the ends of the bars. The *Yes* bar is a little more than 90, or about 92. The *No* bar is a little less than 60, or about 58.

Subtract to find the difference. $92 - 58 = 34$

There are **34 more** *Yes* votes than *No* votes.

Data Analysis Practice 3

A. Questions 1–4 refer to the bar graph below.

1. What is the travel speed on the fastest route?

2. Which roadway has the lowest travel speed?

3. How much faster is the travel speed on Route 2 than on US 101?

4. Kim can take either the Beltway or Route 2 to work. If the distances are the same, which route is likely to get her there faster?

The morning news uses this graph to show rush-hour travel speeds on major routes.

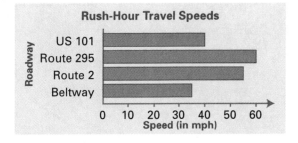

B. Questions 5–8 refer to the double-bar graph below.

5. Which department has 5 more women than men?

6. How many employees in all work in sales?

7. How many more men are there in manufacturing than women?

8. How many total employees work at this company?

This graph shows the employees in each department of R & S Manufacturing.

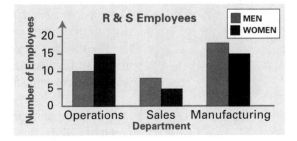

C. Solve each problem. Then choose the correct answer.

9. How many stores in the mall sell clothes or shoes?

   (1) 5
   (2) 10
   (3) 15
   (4) 19
   (5) 20

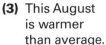

10. Based on the data in the graph, what conclusion would you most likely make about the weather this August?

   (1) This August is drier than average.
   (2) This August is wetter than average.
   (3) This August is warmer than average.
   (4) This August is cooler than average.
   (5) This August is stormier than average.

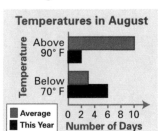

Answers and explanations start on page 89.

**How to Read
Line Graphs**

Line graphs show changes in data over time. A line graph has two different scales, one on each axis. Points are plotted at the intersection of values from the vertical and horizontal axes.

The graph below shows a company's weekly closing stock price for 6 weeks. What was the closing price on week 6?

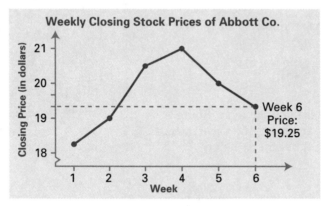

Find the point directly above week 6.
Look across to the vertical axis. The closing price was **$19.25.**

Spot Trends

The line that connects points on the graph can help you predict trends, or patterns of change, in the data. In the graph above, the stock prices continued to rise from week 1 to week 4. Then the prices fell for weeks 5 and 6. Because the prices fell from week 4 to week 6 and depending on the reason for the trend, you would not expect a sharp increase for week 7.

**Explore Double-
Line Graphs**

Double-line graphs are used to compare similar data sets. You can study the graph to look for similarities and differences in trends.

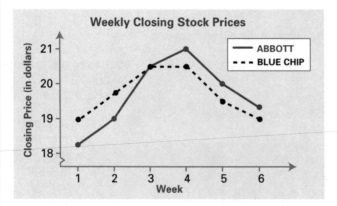

This graph shows that the stock prices of both companies rose and fell at the same time, but the Blue Chip prices were lower than those of the Abbott Company after the first two weeks.

Data Analysis Practice 4

A. Questions 1–4 refer to the line graph below.

1. Between which two years was there no increase in tuition?

2. What was the tuition for year 5?

3. About how much did the tuition increase from year 1 to year 6?

4. How would you describe the change in tuition during the 6-year period?

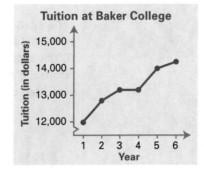

B. Questions 5–8 refer to the double-line graph below.

5. At the beginning of which month were the checking and savings balances equal?

6. What is the difference between the account balances in February?

7. How would you describe the changes in the checking account balance during these months?

8. What trend do you see for the savings account balance?

C. Solve each problem. Then choose the correct answer.

9. In the first graph above, which would be the best estimate for tuition in year 7?

   (1) $13,200
   (2) $14,000
   (3) $14,800
   (4) $20,000
   (5) $25,000

10. Using the double-line graph above, what would be a reasonable prediction for Tom's savings balance at the end of July?

   (1) $500   **(4)** $900
   (2) $680   **(5)** $1,000
   (3) $800

11. What is a reasonable explanation for the population trend shown below?

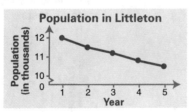

   (1) The school system got a high rating.
   (2) A company in town just hired 500 people.
   (3) The town announced a tax decrease.
   (4) Home construction has increased.
   (5) A major employer has moved out of state.

Answers and explanations start on page 89.

Interpret Scatter Plots

A scatter plot is another kind of graph that shows the relationship between two sets of data. Points on the graph are plotted like coordinate pairs. A line of best fit can be drawn that passes through or close to most of the points. The line is used to make predictions.

The scatter plot below shows the correlation (relationship) between latitude of selected cities and their average January temperature. The equator is at 0° latitude. Latitude numbers are greater for cities located farther north from the equator. What would the average January temperature be for a selected city at 44°N latitude?

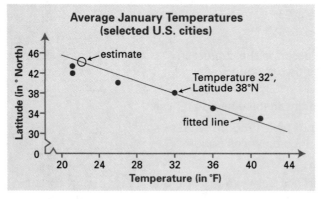

Find 44°N latitude on the vertical axis. Look directly across to the line of best fit, then follow directly down to the horizontal axis. You can estimate an average January temperature of 21° at 44°N latitude.

Identify Central Tendencies

Scatter plots can be used to generalize how data in a set compares. The graph can show a positive correlation, a negative correlation, or no correlation.

The data set above has a negative correlation. As you move right, the line of best fit slopes down. As latitude numbers <u>increase</u>, temperatures <u>decrease</u>.

This scatter plot shows the relationship between the time Scott spends studying and the grades he gets on tests.

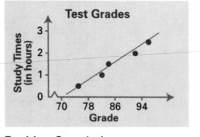

Positive Correlation

This scatter plot shows the relationship between the restaurant prices and calories for different meals.

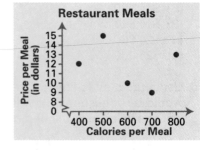

No Correlation

The closer the points are to the fitted line, the stronger the correlation. The farther the points are from the fitted line, the weaker the correlation.

Data Analysis Practice 5

A. Tell whether each scatter plot shows a *negative correlation*, *positive correlation*, or *no correlation*. If there is a correlation, write *strong* or *weak*.

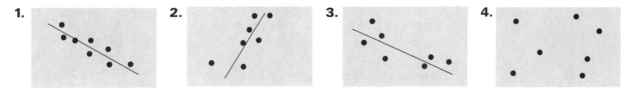

1.   2.   3.   4.

B. Questions 5–8 refer to the scatter plot below.

5. What is the length of the fish that weighs 40 pounds?

This scatter plot shows the length and weight of several different fish.

6. Would you describe this correlation as negative or positive? Strong or weak?

7. How does the length of a striped bass relate to its weight?

8. What is a reasonable estimate for the length of a bass that weighs 35 pounds?

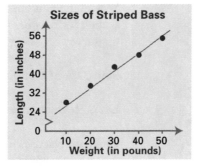

C. Solve each problem. Then choose the correct answer.

9. Which of these phrases best describes the correlation in this scatter plot?

   (1) no correlation
   (2) negative correlation, weak
   (3) negative correlation, strong
   (4) positive correlation, weak
   (5) positive correlation, strong

10. What would you predict would be the number of air conditioners sold on a day with a temperature of about 90?

   (1) 12
   (2) 14
   (3) 18
   (4) 24
   (5) 26

This scatter plot shows how many air conditioners were sold on different days.

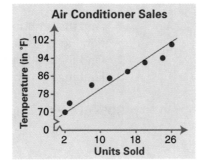

Answers and explanations start on page 89.

Analyze Circle Graphs

Circle graphs represent parts of a whole. The individual sections show the parts.

An advertising company is planning a campaign for Active Feet Sneaker Company. The ad company conducts a survey of 1,000 customers. Which reason did about $\frac{1}{4}$ of the customers select for buying Active Feet Sneakers?

Why Buy Active Foot Sneakers

Comfort/Fit **37%**
Price **11%**
Quality **28%**
Brand Loyalty **24%**

Each section of the graph is labeled with a reason for buying the sneakers and the percentage of customers who stated this reason. The size of each section represents the percent of the total.

To find which section is about $\frac{1}{4}$ of the total, look at the percents. The fraction $\frac{1}{4}$ is equal to 25%. The section for **brand loyalty** shows 24%. This is about $\frac{1}{4}$ of the total.

When circle graphs show percents, you can calculate specific numbers. The section for *comfort/fit* in the graph shows 37%. There were 1,000 customers in the survey.

Find 37% of 1,000. $0.37 \times 1,000 = 370$

So, **370 customers** buy the sneakers for comfort or fit.

Parts of a Whole

Circle graphs use different ways to represent parts of a whole. Graphs can show percents, fractions, decimals, whole numbers, or even dollar amounts. The graph below is labeled with dollar amounts.

This graph shows how the fire department spends its budget.

What percent of the budget is spent on fire fighting?

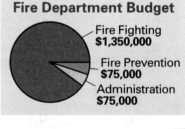

Fire Department Budget

Fire Fighting **$1,350,000**
Fire Prevention **$75,000**
Administration **$75,000**

1. Find the amount spent on fire fighting. $1,350,000
2. Find the total budget. $1,350,000 + $75,000 + $75,000 = $1,500,000
3. Find the percent of the total. 1,350,000 ÷ 1,500,000 = 0.9 = 90%

90% of the fire department budget is spent on fighting fires.

Data Analysis Practice 6

A. Questions 1–4 refer to the graph below.

1. The Northeast representatives make up what percent of the total sales force?

2. Which two regions make up half of the total sales force?

3. What part of the total sales force is located in the Northwest region? Write the number as a decimal.

4. What fraction of the sales force works in the Midwest?

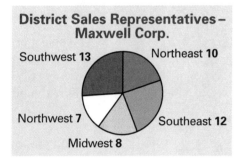

District Sales Representatives – Maxwell Corp.

Southwest **13** Northeast **10**
Northwest **7** Southeast **12**
Midwest **8**

B. Questions 5–8 refer to the graph below.

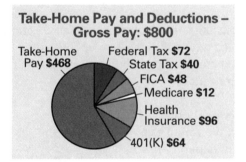

Take-Home Pay and Deductions – Gross Pay: $800

Take-Home Pay **$468**
Federal Tax **$72**
State Tax **$40**
FICA **$48**
Medicare **$12**
Health Insurance **$96**
401(K) **$64**

5. What is the total amount of deductions? (Hint: Take-home pay is not a deduction.)

6. What percent of gross pay does this employee invest in a 401(K) account?

7. What percent of gross pay is deducted for state and federal taxes?

8. What percent of gross pay does this employee contribute for health insurance?

C. Solve each problem. Then choose the correct answer.

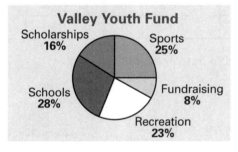

Valley Youth Fund

Scholarships **16%**
Sports **25%**
Schools **28%**
Fundraising **8%**
Recreation **23%**

9. Which item receives the greatest amount of money?

(1) schools
(2) sports
(3) fund-raising
(4) recreation
(5) scholarships

10. If the fund has a total of $10,000, how much is spent on schools?

(1) $280
(2) $1,600
(3) $2,300
(4) $2,500
(5) $2,800

11. One year the fund raised $20,000. How much of this amount was for sports and recreation?

(1) $15,200
(2) $10,200
(3) $9,600
(4) $5,000
(5) $4,600

Answers and explanations start on page 90.

PROBABILITY, PART I

Simple Probability

Probability is the chance of certain events happening.

Probability is written as a fraction.

$$\text{Probability of an event} = \frac{\text{number of favorable outcomes}}{\text{number of possible outcomes}}$$

If you select one card from a full deck of playing cards, what is the probability that it will be a 10?

1. Find the number of favorable outcomes.

How many 10s are in a full deck of cards? (4)

2. Find the total number, or possible outcomes.

How many cards are in a full deck? (52)

3. Write the ratio of favorable outcomes to possible outcomes.

$$\frac{4}{52} = \frac{1}{13}$$

The probability of selecting a 10 is **1 out of 13**, or $\frac{1}{13}$.

Experimental Probability

Probability can be based on the outcome of an experiment. In an experiment, the action is repeated several times, and the results are recorded. Each time the action is repeated is a trial. The experimental probability is written as a ratio of favorable outcomes to the number of trials.

In the game Double Ten, players get bonus points each time they get 10 on the roll of two number cubes. Erin performs an experiment to find the experimental probability of rolling a 10. The table shows the numbers she rolled in each of the 24 trials.

| 7 | 4 | 12 | 6 | 11 | 2 | 8 | 6 | 10 | 8 | 7 | 8 |
| 9 | 10 | 5 | 9 | 7 | 3 | 2 | 4 | 5 | 6 | 11 | 4 |

1. Find the number of favorable outcomes (roll of 10).

2

2. Find the number of trials.

24

3. Write the ratio of favorable outcomes to number of trials.

$$\frac{2}{24} = \frac{1}{12}$$

The experimental probability of rolling a 10 is $\frac{1}{12}$.

Data Analysis Practice 7

A. Find each probability.

1. What is the probability of selecting *red* from box 1?

2. What is the probability of selecting a number greater than 6 from box 2?

3. What is the probability of selecting a number less than 6 from box 2?

4. What is the probability of selecting white from box 1?

Players pick a card from each box to determine the section (white or red) and number of spaces to move for a game.

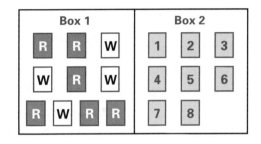

B. Find the experimental probability.

5. What is the probability of selecting a green jelly bean?

6. What is the probability of selecting a black or white jelly bean?

7. What is the probability of selecting a red jelly bean?

8. What is the probability of <u>not</u> selecting a red jelly bean?

A bag contains black (B), white (W), green (G), and red (R) jelly beans. A jelly bean is picked from the bag without looking and then replaced. The color selections for 50 trials are shown here.

B	R	R	B	W	G	G	R	W	B
R	G	W	R	W	B	G	G	R	W
W	B	R	R	W	W	G	B	W	R
B	G	R	G	W	R	B	W	R	W
R	R	B	G	B	W	R	W	R	G

C. Solve each problem. Then choose the correct answer.

The spinner below has 12 equal sections.

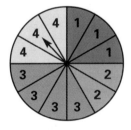

9. What is the probability of spinning a 1?

(1) $\frac{1}{3}$ (4) $\frac{1}{5}$

(2) $\frac{3}{10}$ (5) $\frac{1}{12}$

(3) $\frac{1}{4}$

10. If a player spins a 2, she wins. What is the probability of spinning a 2?

(1) $\frac{1}{12}$ (4) $\frac{1}{3}$

(2) $\frac{1}{6}$ (5) $\frac{3}{5}$

(3) $\frac{1}{5}$

11. If a player spins a 4, he will lose a turn. What is the probability of not spinning a 4?

(1) $\frac{1}{9}$ (4) $\frac{3}{4}$

(2) $\frac{1}{4}$ (5) $\frac{9}{10}$

(3) $\frac{1}{3}$

Answers and explanations start on page 90.

Independent Events

Some probability situations involve two actions or events. Two events are independent if the first event <u>does not</u> affect the outcome of the second event. In the example below, the selection of a name does not affect the probability of selecting a particular topic.

In biology, students are doing projects on different kinds of plants. To assign topics, the teacher puts slips of paper with the students' names in one bag and topics in another bag. There are 8 males and 8 females in the class, and there are 16 different topics. What is the probability of a female with the topic *coniferous trees*?

1. Find the probability of the first event (8 females out of 16 students).
$$\frac{8}{16} = \frac{1}{2}$$

2. Find the probability of the second event (1 out of 16 topics).
$$\frac{1}{16}$$

3. Multiply to find the probability of both events.
$$\frac{1}{2} \times \frac{1}{16} = \frac{1}{32}$$

The probability of selecting *female* and *coniferous trees* is $\frac{1}{32}$.

Depcendent Events

Two events are dependent if the result of the first event does affect the second event.

Game show contestants pick two number balls at random. There are four balls each for the numbers 1–4. A contestant selects a ball, holds it, and then selects a second ball. What is the probability of selecting a 2 and then a 3?

Category	1	2	3	4
Questions	1 1 1 1 2 2 2 2 3 3 3 3 4 4 4 4			

1. Find the probability of the first event (4 balls with number 2 out of 16 balls).
$$\frac{4}{16} = \frac{1}{4}$$

2. Find the probability of the second event. Since 1 ball has been picked, there are now 15 balls (4 balls with the number 3 out of 15 balls).
$$\frac{4}{15}$$

3. Multiply to find the probability of both events.
$$\frac{1}{4} \times \frac{4}{15} = \frac{1}{15}$$

The probability of picking a 2 and then a 3 is $\frac{1}{15}$.

Data Analysis Practice 8

A. Tell whether the events are *independent* or *dependent*.

1. A child randomly selects one pencil and then a second pencil from a bucket full of different-color pencils.

2. One cooler has different-flavored juice boxes. Another cooler has different-flavored ice-cream cups. A person picks one juice box and one ice-cream cup.

3. A player picks one card from a full deck and then another card from a different full deck.

4. A box holds six different-color lollipops. A person picks one and then a second lollipop.

B. Find each probability.

5. A player spins the spinner and tosses a number cube. What is the probability of getting *blue* and a *6* as a result?

6. Gina spins the spinner two times in a row. What is the probability of spinning *yellow* both times?

7. Marco tosses the number cube and spins the spinner. What is the probability that he tosses a number greater than 3 and spins *yellow* or *green*?

8. A player tosses a number cube twice. What is the probability of tossing either a 1 or a 2 both times?

This spinner is used in a game with a cube labeled with the numbers 1–6.

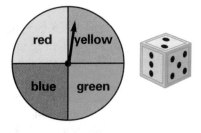

C. Solve each problem. Then choose the correct answer.

9. For a raffle, 50 tickets are sold. The first ticket pulled from the box wins first prize. After the first prize is picked, what is the probability of any ticket left being picked for second prize?

(1) $\frac{1}{25}$

(2) $\frac{1}{50}$

(3) $\frac{1}{49}$

(4) $\frac{1}{99}$

(5) $\frac{1}{2,500}$

10. Look at problem 3 above. Which expression can be used to find the probability of picking a 7 from both decks?

(1) $\frac{1}{52} \times \frac{1}{52}$ **(4)** $\frac{1}{7} \times \frac{1}{7}$

(2) $\frac{1}{13} \times \frac{1}{13}$ **(5)** $\frac{1}{13} + \frac{1}{13}$

(3) $4 \div 52$

11. At the grand opening of Kent's Department Store, shoppers randomly pick one scratch card for each $50 they spend. The coupons can be used for purchases in May. The cards below are in a box.

What is the probability of one customer picking two *20% off purchase* tickets from the box?

(1) $\frac{29}{330}$ **(4)** $\frac{9}{100}$

(2) $\frac{2}{5}$ **(5)** $\frac{1}{30}$

(3) $\frac{1}{9}$

Answers and explanations start on page 90.

GED Skill Builder

THE FIVE-STEP STRATEGY

To solve word problems, you need to have a strategy for how to approach and solve the problem. The five-step strategy uses this approach.

STEP 1. Read and understand the problem.
STEP 2. Find the necessary facts and information.
STEP 3. Choose the correct operations.
STEP 4. Solve the problem.
STEP 5. Check your answer to make sure it makes sense.

Sample Question

Arlo's goal is to save $1,200. If he saves $150 each month for 5 months, how much more does he need to save to reach his goal?

(1) $150
(2) $450
(3) $750
(4) $1,200
(5) $1,950

Think It Through

Q: What is the question asking?
A: The question asks how much more money Arlo needs to save to reach his goal.

Q: What facts do you need to solve the problem?
A: You need the amount being saved each month ($150), the number of months (5), and the total amount to be saved ($1,200).

Q: In this multi-step problem, which operations should you use: addition, subtraction, multiplication, or division?
A: Since Arlo plans to save the same amount for 5 months, you should multiply. Then subtract the amount from the total he wants to save.

Q: Solve the problem. Which answer choice is correct?
A: Choice 1 ($150) is the amount he saves each month.
Choice 2 is correct.
Choice 3 ($750) is not the final answer.
Choice 4 ($1,200) is the total amount Arlo wants to save.
Choice 5 ($1,950) adds instead of subtracts the 5-month total.

Q: Does the answer make sense?
A: Yes, the answer makes sense. Since the amount Arlo already saved ($750) is more than half, the amount left to save should be less than half.

Answer and Explanation

(2) $450 To find the amount Arlo saved over 5 months, multiply $150 by 5. $150 \times 5 = $750. Subtract that amount from Arlo's savings goal: $1,200 - $750 = $450.

Some word problems may have extra information. Other problems may not have all of the facts you need or enough information to calculate the missing facts. For problems that don't have enough information, choose answer choice (5) Not enough information is given.

Sample Question

Arlo's goal this year is to save $1,200. So far, he has saved $150 a month for 5 months. If Arlo meets his goal, how much more will he save this year than he saved last year?

(1) $150
(2) $450
(3) $750
(4) $1,200
(5) Not enough information is given.

Think It Through

Q: What is the question asking?
A: The question asks how much more money Arlo will save this year than he saved last year.

Q: What facts or information do you need to solve the problem?
A: You need to know Arlo's savings goal for this year ($1,200) and the amount he saved last year. The problem does not tell you how much he saved last year, so you cannot answer the question.

Answer and Explanation

(5) Not enough information is given. There is no way to figure out how much money Arlo saved last year. Therefore, choice 5 is correct.

GED Practice

Use the hints to help you solve the problems, and explain your answers.

HINT: Which operations should you use? In what order?

1. A spinach salad costs $4.95. Salad extras cost $1.95 each. What is the cost, before tax, of a spinach salad with two extras?

(1) $1.95   (4) $6.90
(2) $3.95   (5) $8.85
(3) $4.95

Answer _____ is correct because _____

HINT: What facts do you need to solve the problem? Do you have all the facts that you need?

2. An account balance is $465.28. What is the balance after making a deposit of $600 and writing a check for $275.13?

(1) $190.15   (4) $1,340.41
(2) $790.15   (5) Not enough information is given.
(3) $1,065.28

Answer _____ is correct because _____

Answers and explanations start on page 90.

W O R D   P R O B L E M S

Choose the correct answer. Use the hints to help you solve the problems.

1. Ms. Abbott's gross pay is $600, and her take-home pay is $480. The deductions are what percent of Ms. Abbott's gross pay?

THINK: Which operation would you use to find a deduction?

(1) 20%
(2) 25%
(3) 80%
(4) 120%
(5) 125%

2. During a tornado, winds reached 165 miles per hour. According to the table, how is this tornado classified?

Type	Wind Speed (in mph)	Type	Wind Speed (in mph)
F0	<73	F4	207–260
F1	73–112	F5	261–318
F2	113–157	F6	>318
F3	158–206		

THINK: What numbers and digits do you compare to find the answer?

(1) F1
(2) F2
(3) F3
(4) F4
(5) F5

3. A department store will take 10% off of a customer's first purchase if he or she opens a new charge account. What would the cost be for a purchase of $149.50 after 10% is deducted?

THINK: What calculation do you need to do first? What comes next?

(1) $14.95
(2) $134.55
(3) $139.50
(4) $164.45
(5) Not enough information is given.

4. Brett is buying a car for a total cost of $11,580. The car manufacturer offers a loan deal with 0% interest for 5 years. Brett will pay the loan in equal monthly payments. What will his monthly payment be?

THINK: What is the total number of payments?

(1) $2,316.00
(2) $965.00
(3) $241.25
(4) $193.00
(5) $19.30

5. Mr. Romero bought $2\frac{1}{8}$ pounds of apples and $3\frac{3}{4}$ pounds of oranges. He also bought two pears and a bunch of grapes that weighed $1\frac{1}{2}$ pounds. How many pounds of fruit did Mr. Romero buy in all?

THINK: What information about each kind of fruit do you need to know to solve the problem?

(1) $7\frac{1}{4}$ pounds
(2) $7\frac{3}{8}$ pounds
(3) $7\frac{7}{8}$ pounds
(4) $9\frac{3}{4}$ pounds
(5) Not enough information is given.

6. Last year Vega Construction Company made a profit of $80,000. This year, the company's profit was $88,000. What was the rate of change in profits from last year to this year?

THINK: What is the original number that the change is compared to?

(1) 1% increase
(2) 9% increase
(3) 10% increase
(4) 91% increase
(5) 10% decrease

Choose the one best answer to each question.

7. These folders are on Carson's computer. Which answer choice lists the folder size in order from greatest to least?

Size: 3.29 MB   Size: 4.2 MB

Size: 4.14 MB   Size: 4.02 MB

(1) B, C, D, A
(2) C, D, B, A
(3) C, B, D, A
(4) A, D, B, C
(5) C, B, A, D

8. Some magazines send out free copies to key people to increase circulation numbers for advertising purposes. One magazine has 14,904 paid subscriptions and 1,242 free subscriptions. What is the ratio of paid subscriptions to free subscriptions?

(1) 12 to 1
(2) 1 to 12
(3) 11 to 1
(4) 1 to 11
(5) Not enough information is given.

9. A large jar of tomato sauce has a weight of 1.27 kilograms. A case of sauce includes six jars. What is the total weight of a case of tomato sauce, in kilograms?

(1) 4.73
(2) 6.00
(3) 6.22
(4) 7.27
(5) 7.62

10. Mr. Chung needs to buy some wire, and it must have a diameter between 0.45 and 0.5 centimeter. If the following diameters are listed in centimeters, which of the following diameters could he use?

(1) 0.366
(2) 0.406
(3) 0.447
(4) 0.488
(5) 0.538

11. Below is an invoice for home heating oil. What amount belongs in the blank?

INVOICE	
Account No. 1065	
DESCRIPTION	AMOUNT
#2 OIL 122.4 gallons at $1.30 per gallon	
PLEASE PAY THIS AMOUNT	?

(1) $48.96   (4) $252.40
(2) $159.02   (5) $1,591.20
(3) $159.12

12. Sheila bought a parcel of land for $12,000. She gave the owner $2,000 and agreed to pay the remaining amount in equal monthly payments. What will the monthly payments be?

(1) $10,000
(2) $5,000
(3) $500
(4) $400
(5) Not enough information is given.

13. Rodney had $3\frac{1}{2}$ gallons of paint. He used $\frac{1}{4}$ of this amount on a job. How many gallons of paint did Rodney use on the job?

(1) $\frac{7}{8}$
(2) $1\frac{1}{8}$
(3) $3\frac{1}{4}$
(4) $3\frac{3}{4}$
(5) 14

Answers and explanations start on page 90.

MULTI-STEP PROBLEMS

Some word problems require several steps, often involving more than one operation. Use the five-step approach with multi-step problems.

STEP 1. Read and understand the problem.
STEP 2. Find the necessary facts and information.
STEP 3. Choose the correct operations.
STEP 4. Solve the problem.
STEP 5. Check your answer to make sure it makes sense.

Sample Question

Investments earn different rates of interest. What would be the difference in interest earned on $15,000 for 1 year at a rate of 5% and 1 year at a rate of 7%?

(1) $300
(2) $750
(3) $1,050
(4) $1,300
(5) $1,800

Think It Through

Q: What is the question asking?
A: The question asks for the difference in interest earned for 1 year at two different rates.

Q: What facts do you need to solve the problem?
A: You need the amount of the investment ($15,000) and the two different interest rates (5% and 7%).

Q: Which operations should you use and in what order?
A: First use multiplication to find the amount of interest earned at each different rate. Then subtract the two interest amounts.

Q: Solve the problem. Which answer choice is correct?
A: **Choice 1 is correct.**
Choice 2 ($750) is the interest earned at 5%.
Choice 3 ($1,050) is the interest earned at 7%.
Choice 4 ($1,300) incorrectly subtracts the two amounts.
Choice 5 ($1,800) adds instead of subtracts the two amounts.

Q: Does the answer make sense?
A: Yes, the answer makes sense. The problem looks for a difference, and the answer is considerably less than each amount of interest.

Answer and Explanation

(1) $300 To find the amount earned at 5%, multiply 0.05 by $15,000. $0.05 \times \$15,000 = \$750$. To find the amount earned at 7%, multiply 0.07 by $15,000. $0.07 \times \$15,000 = \$1,050$. Subtract the two amounts to find the difference: $\$1,050 - \$750 = \$300$.

Another approach would be to find the difference in the two interest rates ($7\% - 5\% = 2\%$). Then find 2% of the investment ($\$15,000 \times 0.02 = \$300$).

Some multi-step problems ask you to find the correct setup for solving a problem without performing the calculations necessary to get the final answer. To do this, you must determine the steps needed to solve the problem. It is also important to think about the order of operations.

Sample Question

The lunch buffet at the Shore Cafe is $8 for adults and $5 for children under 12 years old. Which expression shows the buffet cost for a group of 4 adults and 10 children under 12 years old?

(1) $8 + $5
(2) $8 × 4
(3) $5 × 10
(4) ($8 + $5) × 14
(5) ($8 × 4) + ($5 × 10)

Think It Through

Q: What is the question asking?
A: The question asks which expression can be used to find the cost of 4 adults' and 10 children's meals.

Q: What facts or information do you need to solve the problem?
A: You need to know the number of adults (4), the price for adults ($8), the number of children (10), and the price for children ($5).

Answer and Explanation

(5) ($8 × 4) + ($5 × 10) This shows the product of the price of an adult meal times the number of adults, then adds the product to the price of a children's meal times the number of children.

Guided Practice

Use the hints to help you solve the problems, and explain your answers.

HINT: Which operations should you use? In what order?

1. Large boxes hold 24 books, and small boxes hold 8 books. How many books are in a shipment of 10 large boxes and 2 small boxes?

(1) 18   **(4)** 240
(2) 16   **(5)** 256
(3) 224

Answer _____ is correct because _____

HINT: Which operation should you do first? What facts do you need to solve the problem?

2. A company has 6 full-time and 2 part-time workers. Full-time workers get a $100 bonus, and part-time workers get a $50 bonus. Which expression shows the total bonus money given to employees?

(1) (6 × 2) + ($100 × $50)   **(4)** (6 × $100) × (2 × $50)
(2) (6 × $50) + (2 × $100)   **(5)** (6 + $100) × (2 + $50)
(3) (6 × $100) + (2 × $50)

Answer _____ is correct because _____

Answers and explanations start on page 91.

Choose the correct answer. Use the hints to help you solve the problems.

1. A 20-ounce box of Oat Flakes costs $3.29, and a 13-ounce box sells for $2.49. Which expression can be used to find the unit price difference for the two boxes of cereal?

   THINK: Which operation do you use to find unit price?

   (1) $3.29 − $2.49
   (2) ($3.29 × 20) − ($2.49 × 13)
   (3) ($2.49 ÷ 13) − ($3.29 ÷ 20)
   (4) ($3.29 ÷ 20) + ($2.49 ÷ 13)
   (5) $\dfrac{\$3.29 \div 20}{\$2.49 \div 13}$

2. Carrie orders some camping supplies from a catalog. She buys two flashlights for $19.99, a backpack for $39.99, and a cooler for $24.99. What will be the cost of Carrie's purchase, including shipping?

Total Purchase	Shipping Charge
$0–$50.00	$4.95
$50.01–$100.00	$6.95
$100.01–$150.00	$8.95
over $150.00	$10.95

   THINK: What are the steps needed to solve this problem?

   (1) $84.97
   (2) $91.92
   (3) $104.96
   (4) $112.91
   (5) $113.91

3. A car goes 22 miles on 1 gallon of gas. Which expression shows the cost to take a 176-mile trip at a price of $1.85 per gallon?

   THINK: What calculation do you need to do first?

   (1) (176 ÷ 22) × $1.85
   (2) (176 − 22) × $1.85
   (3) (176 ÷ $1.85) × 22
   (4) 176 × $1.85
   (5) (176 ÷ $1.85) + 22

4. The town of Lincoln has a pay-as-you-throw trash program. Residents pay $7.50 for a package of five large trash bags. If a family uses six large trash bags in a month, what is the monthly cost for trash removal?

   THINK: What is the price for one trash bag?

   (1) $45.00
   (2) $37.50
   (3) $9.00
   (4) $7.50
   (5) $6.25

5. Teresa is going to college this year. Tuition is $8,750 for each of the two semesters. Room and board costs $6,200, and books are $680. If Teresa receives financial aid of $8,220, what will she pay in all for college this year?

   THINK: Which operations are needed to solve this problem?

   (1) $7,410
   (2) $16,160
   (3) $23,850
   (4) $24,380
   (5) $32,600

6. A hurricane is on a direct path to Ace Beach. At 8:00 A.M. on Monday, the storm is 450 miles from Ace Beach, traveling at 15 mph. If it continues on a direct path at the same rate, at what time will the hurricane reach Ace Beach?

   THINK: How can you find the time using the rate and distance?

   (1) 1:00 P.M. on Monday
   (2) 12:00 noon on Tuesday
   (3) 2:00 P.M. on Tuesday
   (4) 1:00 A.M. on Tuesday
   (5) 1:00 P.M. on Tuesday

Choose the one best answer to each question.

7. The Mountainside Hotel charges $79 a night for a room. The state charges a 7% tax for hotel rooms. Which expression shows the cost, with tax, for a 3-night stay at the hotel?

   (1) 0.07 × $79 × 3
   (2) 1.07 × $79 × 3
   (3) $79 × 3 + 7
   (4) $79 + 0.7 × 79
   (5) $79 × 0.7

8. The diagram shows a hiking route. Mark plans to hike this route, and he wants to return no later than 3:00 P.M. He hikes at an average pace of 2 miles per hour. What is the latest time that Mark should plan to begin his hike?

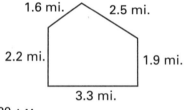

   (1) 8:30 A.M.
   (2) 9:00 A.M.
   (3) 9:10 A.M.
   (4) 9:30 A.M.
   (5) 9:40 A.M.

9. After an accident, Dale had his car repaired. The insurance company covers the cost of the repairs after a $300 deductible. The cost for parts was $545, and the labor charge was $1,200. What was the total amount that the insurance company had to pay for the repairs?

   (1) $300
   (2) $355
   (3) $955
   (4) $1,445
   (5) $2,045

10. Katie bought a dining room set. She made a deposit of $50 and will make monthly payments of $60 for 1 year. Which expression shows the total amount Katie will pay for the dining room set?

   (1) $50 + $60 × 12
   (2) $60 × 12 − $50
   (3) ($50 + $60) × 12
   (4) $60 + $50 × 12
   (5) $50 + $60

11. Mrs. Samuel wants to tile her bathroom floor. She is trying to decide between two tiles, one that costs $2.60 per square foot and the other that costs $2.75 per square foot. What is the price difference to cover the floor with these tiles?

   (1) $0.15
   (2) $3.00
   (3) $14.40
   (4) $249.60
   (5) $264.00

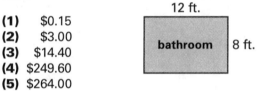

12. A 2-year magazine subscription is $66. The price per monthly issue at a newsstand is $3.49. What is the savings per issue for the subscription rate?

   (1) $0.74
   (2) $1.74
   (3) $2.01
   (4) $2.75
   (5) $17.76

13. Brian bought a car for $2,000, spent $250 on repairs, and sold it for $3,000. Brian's profit is what percent of the original price of the car?

   (1) ($3,000 − $2,000) ÷ $2,000
   (2) ($3,000 − $250) ÷ $2,000
   (3) ($3,000 − $2,000 + $250) ÷ $1,000
   (4) ($3,000 − $2,000 − $250) ÷ $2,000
   (5) ($3,000 + $2,000 − $250) ÷ $2,000

Answers and explanations start on page 91.

**DECIMALS
AND THE
CALCULATOR**

On parts of the GED Mathematics Test, you will use a calculator. Here are some of the keys you should know on the Casio *fx*-260 calculator.

fraction key →

→ operation keys

decimal point →

Sample Question

Subtract: $345.18 − $102.38

(1) $241.80
(2) $242.08
(3) $242.80
(4) $447.56
(5) $24,280.00

Think It Through

Q: What keys should you press?
A: Press 3 4 5 ⌷·⌷ 1 8 ⌷−⌷ 1 0 2 ⌷·⌷ 3 8 ⌷=⌷. The display shows 242.8.

Q: How do you read the display?
A: The calculator display does not include zeros at the end of a number. Since the problem involves money, the answer is 242 dollars and 80 cents.

Q: How do you write the answer?
A: Include the 0 at the end and use a dollar sign: $242.80.

Q: Solve the problem. Which answer choice is correct?
A: Choice 1($241.80) is one dollar less.
Choice 2 ($242.08) has the 0 and 8 in the wrong places.
Choice 3 is correct.
Choice 4 ($447.56) adds instead of subtracts the two amounts.
Choice 5 ($24,280.00) did not use decimal points.

Answer and
Explanation

(3) $242.80 If you use the calculator to find the difference of $345.18 − $102.38, the display shows 242.8, which is $242.80.

FRACTIONS AND THE CALCULATOR

Sample Question

You can use the Casio *fx*-260 calculator to compute with fractions. Use the fraction key to enter the numbers.

Multiply: $\frac{1}{2} \times 3\frac{2}{3}$

(1) $\frac{5}{6}$ **(4)** $\frac{15}{6}$

(2) $1\frac{1}{6}$ **(5)** $4\frac{1}{6}$

(3) $1\frac{5}{6}$

Think It Through

Q: What keys should you press?
A: Press 1 $\boxed{a^{b/}c}$ 2 $\boxed{\times}$ 3 $\boxed{a^{b/}c}$ 2 $\boxed{a^{b/}c}$ 3 $\boxed{=}$. The display shows $\boxed{1\rfloor5\rfloor6}$.

Q: How do you read the display?
A: The $\rfloor$ appears between each part of the fraction or mixed number. This display of $1\rfloor5\rfloor6$ means $1\frac{5}{6}$.

Answer and Explanation

The answer is **(3)** $1\frac{5}{6}$.

Press these keys to calculate, $\frac{1}{2} \times 3\frac{2}{3}$: 1 $\boxed{a^{b/}c}$ 2 $\boxed{\times}$ 3 $\boxed{a^{b/}c}$ 2 $\boxed{a^{b/}c}$ 3 $\boxed{=}$.

The display shows $\boxed{1\rfloor5\rfloor6}$, which is $1\frac{5}{6}$.

Guided Practice

Use the hints to help you solve the problems, and explain your answers.

HINT: What operation should you use to find the amount of the raise?

1. Stan was making $9.72 per hour. After receiving a raise, he now makes $10.45 per hour. What is the amount of the raise?

(1) $20.17   **(4)** $0.73
(2) $7.30   **(5)** $0.72
(3) $0.83

Answer _____ is correct because _____

HINT: Remember to press the fraction key between each part of a mixed number.

2. The dry ingredients in a recipe include $2\frac{1}{4}$ cups of flour and $1\frac{1}{3}$ cups of sugar. How many total cups of flour and sugar are called for?

(1) 1

(2) $2\frac{7}{12}$

(3) 3

(4) $3\frac{5}{12}$

(5) $3\frac{7}{12}$

Answer _____ is correct because _____

Answers and explanations start on page 91.

Choose the correct answer. Use the hints to help you solve the problems. You may use a calculator.

1. A painter spent $\frac{3}{4}$ hour preparing the work area. She then took $4\frac{1}{2}$ hours to paint. What was the total number of hours spent on the job?

THINK: Which operation would you use here to find a total?

(1) $3\frac{3}{4}$

(2) $4\frac{3}{4}$

(3) $5\frac{1}{4}$

(4) $5\frac{1}{2}$

(5) $6\frac{1}{4}$

2. The average monthly rainfall in Greenfield for June is 3.6 inches. This June, Greenfield received 5.2 inches of rain. How does the rainfall this June compare to the average?

THINK: Which is greater, the average or the amount for this year?

(1) 0.6 inch above average
(2) 1.4 inches above average
(3) 1.5 inches above average
(4) 1.6 inches above average
(5) 1.6 inches below average

3. Below is the summary section of a telephone bill. What amount belongs in the BALANCE box?

```
Account # 8490256

Digital Phone Service        $54.23
Long-Distance Services       $ 1.48
Package Savings             −$12.50

BALANCE                    [        ]
```

THINK: Which operations do you need to use?

(1) $41.73
(2) $43.21
(3) $55.71
(4) $65.25
(5) $66.73

4. A.R. Asphalt Company is paving two roads today. One road is $3\frac{3}{10}$ miles long. The other road is $4\frac{3}{5}$ miles long. What is the total length, in miles, of the roads to be paved?

THINK: Between which numbers will you press the fraction key to enter each mixed number?

(1) $1\frac{3}{10}$

(2) $7\frac{7}{10}$

(3) $7\frac{9}{10}$

(4) $8\frac{1}{10}$

(5) $8\frac{1}{5}$

5. Rhonda lives 6.4 miles from her office. She travels back and forth to work 3 days each week. How many miles does she travel back and forth to work each week?

THINK: What is the first step you need to do to solve the problem?

(1) 9.4
(2) 19.2
(3) 38.4
(4) 38.8
(5) 39.0

6. Salmon is on sale this week for $4.79 per pound. Ramon buys salmon filets with a total weight of 3.5 pounds. How much does he pay for the fish? Remember to round to the nearest cent.

THINK: When entering the numbers on a calculator, pay attention to the placement of the decimal points in each number.

(1) $8.29
(2) $16.73
(3) $16.76
(4) $16.77
(5) $17.12

Choose the one best answer to each question. You may use a calculator.

7. Michael's best time in the 400-meter run is 54.28 seconds. In his last race, Michael beat his record by 8 seconds. What was his time in this race, in seconds?

(1) 46.28
(2) 53.48
(3) 54.20
(4) 54.36
(5) 55.08

8. Three brothers bought a gift for their mother. They each paid an equal amount. How much did each person pay?

(1) $8.23
(2) $8.56
(3) $8.58
(4) $12.84
(5) $22.68

$25.68

9. A contractor received $\frac{1}{4}$ of the total job price as his first payment. He then spent $\frac{1}{3}$ of this amount on materials to frame the job. If the total job price is $17,120, how much was the contractor's first payment?

(1) $1,426.67
(2) $4,280.00
(3) $5,706.67
(4) $12,840.00
(5) $68,480.00

10. A concert lasted $2\frac{1}{2}$ hours. Each band played for $\frac{1}{2}$ hour. How many bands played at the concert?

(1) 2
(2) 4
(3) 5
(4) 8
(5) 10

11. Matt is buying three packages of ground beef for a cookout. The packages weigh 1.38 lb., 1.24 lb., and 1.29 lb. How many pounds of meat is Matt buying?

(1) 2.53   **(4)** 3.90
(2) 2.62   **(5)** 3.91
(3) 2.67

Questions 12 and 13 refer to the diagram.

Board length before cut is 96 inches.

$1\frac{1}{4}$ in. $2\frac{3}{8}$ in.

12. Gayle cuts one end off the board to make a square end. She then measures the length that she needs and cuts off the other end. What is the total length of the pieces she cut off, in inches?

(1) $1\frac{1}{8}$

(2) $2\frac{3}{8}$

(3) $3\frac{3}{8}$

(4) $3\frac{5}{8}$

(5) $3\frac{7}{8}$

13. What is the length of the board Gayle has after making both cuts, in inches?

(1) $91\frac{3}{8}$

(2) $92\frac{3}{8}$

(3) $93\frac{5}{8}$

(4) $94\frac{3}{4}$

(5) $95\frac{3}{8}$

14. In a company, $\frac{5}{8}$ of the employees are women, and $\frac{1}{4}$ of the women are managers. If there are 320 employees, how many women managers are there?

(1) 200
(2) 80
(3) 64
(4) 50
(5) 40

Answers and explanations start on page 91.

WHOLE NUMBERS

Some questions on the GED Mathematics Test include a standard grid for recording the answer. For this type of question, there are no multiple-choice options. Instead, you write the answer and then fill in bubbles on the grid.

Sample Question

At a financial convention, an investment workshop was held on two different days. On the first day, 68 people attended the session. On the second day, 84 people were in attendance. How many people attended the session on both days?

The total number of people who attended the workshop is $68 + 84 = 152$.

Think It Through

Q: What is the first line for?
A: Write your answer in the top row. Be sure to write only one digit or symbol per box.

Q: Where do you write the first digit?
A: You can start the answer in any column. Just be sure your entire answer will fit.

Q: What if my answer has fewer than 5 digits?
A: Any columns that you don't need should be left blank.

Q: What do I do with the second and third rows?
A: Those rows are for fractions and decimals answers.

Q: How do I fill in the bubbles?
A: Look at the digits written in the top row. Fill in the appropriate number in each column.

Answer and Explanation

The grids below show three ways to grid the same answer of **152 people.**

DECIMALS

Sample Question

The standard grid can also be used to write answers that are decimals.

Hana's dry-cleaning bill was $36.90. She paid with two 20-dollar bills. How much did Hana receive back for change?

Two 20-dollar bills is $40.00. To find the amount of change, subtract $36.90 from $40.00.

$40.00 − $36.90 = $3.10

Think It Through

Q: How do I record the answer?

A: Write each digit and the decimal point in each box in the first row. You can start in any box, as long as the complete answer is written. Next, fill in the appropriate bubbles in the column below each digit and decimal point.

Answer and Explanation

The answer **3.10** is shown in the grid above. Since the answer is a dollar amount, an end zero is included. It would also be correct to leave off the zero (3.1). Do not include the dollar sign.

Guided Practice

Use the hints to help you solve the problems.

HINT: In problem 1, how many digits are in the answer? In which box will you start?

HINT: Between which digits does the decimal point go in the answer to problem 2?

1. Dylan has a coupon for $20 off any item over $150. He buys a television set with a price of $249. How many dollars does Dylan pay for the television if he uses the coupon?

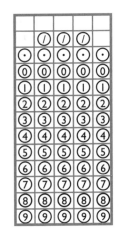

2. A fitness instructor calculated the calories per minute that Helen would burn performing two different kinds of exercise. How many more calories per minute will Helen burn jumping rope than hiking?

Jumping Rope:
11.8 calories per minute
Hiking:
7.2 calories per minute

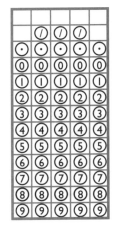

Answers and explanations start on page 92.

Use the hints to help you solve the problems.

1. A company paid $58 per person for a summer outing. If the company has 67 employees, what was the total cost of the outing?

THINK: Do you include dollar signs or commas in the answer?

2. Kelly's test scores are shown below. What is her mean grade?

86, 89, 79, 94, 87, 93

THINK: Which operations do you use to find the mean?

3. The auditorium has 500 seats. During an assembly, there were 20 empty seats. What portion of the total seats was empty? Express the answer as a decimal.

THINK: Where does the decimal point belong in the answer?

4. A credit card company posts a finance charge of 8% on unpaid balances. What would be the charge on an unpaid balance of $325?

THINK: How do you find the part when you know the base and rate?

5. A subway pass costs $42 each month. What would it cost to buy a pass for a whole year?

THINK: What other number do you need to solve the problem?

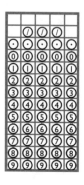

6. Below is a tax bill for a property in the town of Cabot. What would be the total real estate tax assessed for this property?

THINK: What information on the bill shows the tax rate?

TOWN OF CABOT	
Location: 10 Elm St.	
Land Value	$40,000
Building Value	$60,000
Total Value	$100,000
Tax Rate	
Per $1,000	$12.00

7. Tracey bought some fruit to make a berry salad. She bought a 1-pound container of strawberries for $1.88, a 2-pound bunch of grapes for $2.20, and a 12-ounce package of raspberries for $4.75. How much did Tracey pay in all for the fruit?

THINK: Which information is needed to solve the problem?

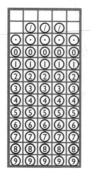

Solve. Mark your answers on the grids.

8. An appliance store charges no interest on purchases paid off within 12 months. Jan buys a refrigerator for $975. She plans to make equal monthly payments. How much must she pay each month so that payment is complete in 12 months?

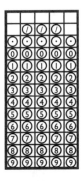

9. The *Daily Times* charges a rate of $3.15 per line for a classified ad for 1 day. What would be the cost to run this ad for 1 day?

> **HANDYMAN SERVICES**
> Small home repairs, painting, and wallpapering. I do both interior and exterior work. Reasonable rates. References provided. Call Roy Ellis at (422) 556-9322.

10. Lionel is driving 1,080 miles to visit his uncle. He plans to take 3 days to make the trip. If Lionel wants to drive an equal distance each day, what is the daily distance he should travel?

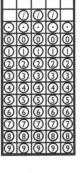

11. A hydroseeding company charges $1.50 per square foot to seed. What would be the cost to seed a lawn that is 275 square feet?

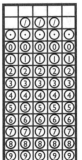

12. Ocean Edge Aquarium has 358 family members, 289 corporate members, and 245 single members. What is the total number of members?

13. A city recreation department sets up an adult soccer league. Enrollment for the league is 180 players. If each team has 12 players, how many teams will there be?

14. Ralph is traveling on an interstate highway. He is at mile marker 76.8. Ralph wants to stop for gas, and sees the sign below. How many miles away is the service area?

> **Next Service Area at Mile 125**

15. A state wildlife organization stocked a lake with 240 trout, 315 bass, and 188 salmon. How many fish were stocked in all?

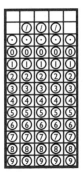

Answers and explanations start on page 92.

PROPER FRACTIONS

On some GED Mathematics Test questions, you will record a fraction answer on the grid. The following example shows how to record a proper fraction on the standard grid.

Sample Question

Arturo spent $\frac{3}{4}$ hour doing math homework. On the same night, his English homework took $\frac{5}{8}$ hour. How much longer did the math homework take than the English homework?

Subtract the English homework time from math homework time.

$$\frac{3}{4} - \frac{5}{8} = \frac{6}{8} - \frac{5}{8} = \frac{1}{8}$$

The math homework took $\frac{1}{8}$ hour longer.

Think It Through

Q: What do you write on the first line?
A: Write your fraction answer in the top row. Use the slash symbol / to indicate the fraction bar.

Q: Where do you write the first digit?
A: You can start the answer in any column. Just be sure that your entire answer will fit.

Q: What is the next step?
A: Look at the digits written in the top row. Fill in the appropriate bubble in each column. Be sure to fill in the / bubble directly under the slash mark you wrote in the top row.

Answer and Explanation

The grids below show three ways to grid the answer. Since there are only two digits and the fraction bar in this answer, you can start in the first, second, or third column. Note that fractions can be entered as decimals on the grid.

$$\frac{1}{8} = 0.125$$

MIXED NUMBERS

Sample Question

The standard grid can also be used to show answers that are mixed numbers.

Jared walked $1\frac{3}{10}$ miles to the library. After checking out some books, Jared walked another $\frac{9}{10}$ mile to his friend's house to work on a project. What is the total distance that Jared walked?

Add the two distances. Write in lowest terms.

$$1\frac{3}{10} + \frac{9}{10} = 1\frac{12}{10} = 2\frac{2}{10} = 2\frac{1}{5}$$

$$2\frac{1}{5} = \frac{11}{5} \text{ miles}$$

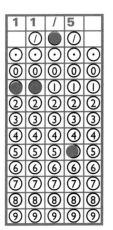

Think It Through

Q: How do I record the answer?

A: You must change the mixed number to an improper fraction. An improper fraction is recorded in the same manner as a proper fraction.

Answer and Explanation

The answer **11/5** is shown in the grid above. Be sure to change $2\frac{1}{5}$ to an improper fraction ($\frac{11}{5}$) to record on the grid. A mixed number on the grid will be scored as incorrect.

Guided Practice

Use the hints to help you solve the problems.

HINT: In problem 1, is the fraction expressed in lowest terms?

HINT: In problem 2, you may want to first change the mixed number to an improper fraction.

1. Leslie works 32 hours a week. While at work, Leslie spends 8 hours a week operating the cash register. What fraction of her work week does Leslie spend at the cash register?

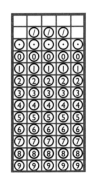

2. A piece of rope is $8\frac{3}{4}$ inches long. The rope is cut into two equal pieces. What is the length of each piece, in inches?

Answers and explanations start on page 92.

Use the hints to help you solve the problems.

1. Of all the games played last season, the Tigers won 48 games, lost 10 games, and tied 2 games. What fraction of the total games did the Tigers win?

   THINK: What is the total number of games played?

2. Ho mixes $\frac{3}{4}$ cup of orange juice with $\frac{1}{3}$ cup of cranberry juice. What is the total number of cups of juice mix he makes?

   THINK: What common denominator should you use?

3. There are 40 tables at the Roadhouse Restaurant. At 6:30, 36 tables were occupied. What fraction of the tables was available at that time?

   THINK: What is the number of tables available at that time?

4. A stack of cat food cans measures 12 inches high. There are 8 cans in the stack. What is the height, in inches, of each can?

   THINK: What operation should you use?

5. The diagram below shows how many of each kind of movie Sean has in his DVD collection. What fraction of the collection is comedy movies?

Science Fiction — 10 DVDs
Mystery — 12 DVDs
Drama — 18 DVDs
Comedy — 60 DVDs

   THINK: What is the first step needed to solve this problem?

6. For her birthday, Julia received a $50 gift card to Marvel Movie Theater. The first time she used the card, Julia spent $15 at the theater. What fraction of the original value of the card is left?

   THINK: What is the dollar value left on the gift card?

7. Jeremy used 40 gallons of gas during a long boat trip. If the boat's gas tank holds 16 gallons, how many tanks of gas did he use?

   THINK: How do you record a mixed number on a standard grid?

Solve each question, and grid in the answer.

8. Below is a diagram of a board that Selena has cut in half to make two equal pieces. If length × width equals area, what is the area of each piece, in feet?

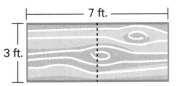
7 ft.

3 ft.

9. A recipe calls for $1\frac{1}{2}$ cups diced potatoes, $\frac{2}{3}$ cup chopped celery, and $\frac{1}{2}$ cup chopped onions. How many cups of vegetables are there in all in the recipe?

10. In a taste test, $\frac{2}{3}$ of the respondents preferred Brand A. Of this group, $\frac{3}{4}$ of the people stated that they regularly buy Brand B. What fraction of the total respondents preferred Brand A but regularly buy Brand B?

11. Carol has two tomato plants in her garden. One plant is $38\frac{3}{4}$ inches tall. The other plant is $36\frac{1}{2}$ inches tall. What is the difference in height between the two plants?

12. Katrina makes canvas bags. Each bag requires $\frac{3}{4}$ yard of material. Katrina gets an order for 6 beige bags. How many yards of material does she need to make the bags for this order?

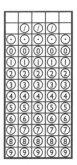

Questions 13 and 14 refer to the graph below.

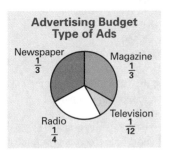

Advertising Budget Type of Ads

Newspaper $\frac{1}{3}$

Magazine $\frac{1}{3}$

Radio $\frac{1}{4}$

Television $\frac{1}{12}$

13. According to the graph, what fraction of the budget is spent on radio ads and newspaper ads?

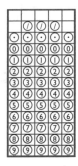

14. How much more of the budget is spent on radio ads than on television ads?

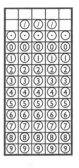

Answers and explanations start on page 92.

NUMBER SENSE, PAGES 12–13

A.

1. $85 > 83$
2. $22 < 55$
3. $104 < 110$
4. $240 < 303$
5. $1,476 = 1,476$
6. $5,213 > 4,768$
7. $12,242 > 11,422$
8. $67,809 < 67,908$
9. $250,000 < 255,000$

B.

10. 23, 25, 28, 29
11. 152, 125, 120, 105
12. 12 lb., 15 lb., 19 lb.
13. 5,277; 5,048; 5,008

C.

14. $x = 1$ through 57
15. $x = 93$ through 150
16. $x = 101, 102, 103, 104, 105$

D.

17. **(4) 21 lb., 18 lb., 12 lb., 9 lb.** To list the boxes in order from heaviest to lightest, compare place values working from left to right.
18. **(3) 35** Only the age 35 is between the ages of 18 and 39. The ages 13 and 17 are too young, and the ages 40 and 45 are too old.
19. **(4) $x = 151$ through 299** The numbers are between 150 and 300, but the group does not include 150 and 300.
20. **(3) Day 3—8,746 tickets** Compare digits from left to right. Since 8,746 and 8,731 have the same hundreds digit, look at the tens place.

ESTIMATION, PAGES 14–15

A.

1. 63,000
2. 4,700
3. 9,000
4. 440,000
5. 5,000,000
6. 30,000
7. 175,000
8. 860

B.

9. $3,100 + 3,400 = 6,500$
10. $3,000,000 + 5,000,000 = 8,000,000$
11. $260,000 - 100,000 = 160,000$
12. $40,000 + 40,000 = 80,000$
13. $500 - 400 = 100$
14. $63,000 - 12,000 = 51,000$

C.

15. **(4) $17,000** To round to the nearest thousand, look at the hundreds place. Since $8 > 5$, round up to the next thousand.
16. **(2) $1,600** Look at the digits in the hundreds place to estimate: $5 + 7 + 4 = 16$. Since these digits are in the hundreds place, the estimate is 1,600.
17. **(1) 34,000,000** Rounded to the millions place, 95,704,000 is 96,000,000. The digit in the hundred thousands place in 62,360,750 is less than 5. The rounded number is 62,000,000. The difference is 34,000,000.

DECIMAL BASICS, PAGES 16–17

A.

1. 2.05
2. 0.102
3. five and eight ten thousandths
4. three thousand nine hundred forty-five ten thousandths
5. 15.6
6. four hundred ninety-five ten thousandths

B.

7. $0.62 > 0.604$
8. $32.05 < 34.92$
9. $0.512 > 0.215$
10. $3.1 = 3.10$
11. $0.898 < 0.988$
12. $56.079 < 59.607$

C.

13. 2.35, 2.39, 2.48, 2.5
14. 3.0, 0.30, 0.03, 0.003
15. 7.2 g, 8.05 g, 8.5 g
16. 0.21, 0.12, 0.102

D.

17. **(3) $19.79** This is the only amount that is between $18.00 and $20.00. $20.02 and $21.00 are greater than $20.00. $17.98 and $16.50 are less than $18.00.
18. **(2) three and forty-eight hundredths** The three is to the left of the decimal point. The last digit on the right is in the hundredths place.
19. **(4) 1939, 1976, 1923, 1920** The order of the numbers from least to greatest is 7.9, 8.0, 8.3, 8.6. These numbers correspond with the dates in choice 4.

ADD AND SUBTRACT DECIMALS, PAGES 18–19

A.

1. $1.65
2. 3.808
3. $65.35
4. 1.743
5. 3,810.78
6. 8.322
7. 66.416
8. 34.083
9. 3.739

B.

10. 26.35
11. 84.375
12. 47.933
13. $260.05

C.

14. **(3) 4.06** The fastest time is 55.04 seconds, and the slowest is 59.10. The difference is 4.06 seconds.
15. **(4) 55.76** The time for Thomas in the chart is 56.56 seconds. Since he took 0.8 second off the time in the chart, subtract: $56.56 - 0.8$.
16. **(5) $177.85** To find the total, add the prices of all three items: $89.95 + $74.95 + $12.95 = $177.85.
17. **(1) 2.45** Subtract the distance Lina has already jogged from the total distance of the route: $8.25 - 5.8 = 2.45$.

MULTIPLY AND DIVIDE DECIMALS, PAGES 20–21

A.

1. 2.88
2. 3.2
3. 73.2036
4. 138
5. 2.007
6. 19.2348

B.

7. $0.05
8. $117.18
9. 0.1533
10. 42.6
11. $316.50
12. 13.89

C.

13. **(2) $0.05** Divide the price of the bottle by the ounces in the bottle: $1.80 ÷ 36 = $0.05.

14. **(4) 21.25** Multiply the distance per day by the number of days: 4.25 × 5 = 21.25.

15. **(3) 8** Divide the width of the box by the diameter of a baseball to see how many balls will fit: 42 ÷ 5.25 = 8.

16. **(4) $11.94** Multiply the price per pound by the number of pounds, and then round the product to the nearest cent: $2.79 × 4.28 = 11.9412, or $11.94 rounded to the nearest cent.

FRACTION BASICS, PAGES 22–23

A.

1. $\frac{21}{9}$ **3.** $\frac{10}{12}$

2. $\frac{7}{10}$ **4.** $\frac{10}{4}$

B.

5. $\frac{43}{10}$ **8.** $1\frac{5}{12}$

6. $\frac{28}{5}$ **9.** $4\frac{2}{3}$

7. $3\frac{1}{4}$ **10.** $\frac{23}{6}$

C.

11. $\frac{7}{8} > \frac{3}{8}$ **14.** $\frac{3}{3} < \frac{5}{3}$

12. $\frac{11}{12} < \frac{17}{12}$ **15.** $\frac{1}{6} < \frac{5}{6}$

13. $\frac{3}{2} = 1\frac{1}{2}$ **16.** $1\frac{1}{10} = \frac{11}{10}$

D.

17. **(3) $1\frac{1}{4}$** Filling a $\frac{1}{4}$ cup 5 times is the same as $\frac{5}{4}$, and $\frac{5}{4}$ can be expressed as the mixed number $1\frac{1}{4}$.

18. **(5) $\frac{1}{8}$** Eliminate (1) since it is greater than 1 and the others are all less than 1. Compare the numerators to find that $\frac{1}{8}$ is the smallest.

19. **(5) Chung** Eliminate (3) because the distance $7\frac{1}{8}$ has the smallest whole number part. Since the other mixed numbers all have the same whole number part, compare the fractions. The greatest is $8\frac{9}{10}$.

EQUIVALENT FRACTIONS, PAGES 24–25

A.

1. $\frac{5}{6}$ **7.** $\frac{7}{8}$

2. $\frac{3}{4}$ **8.** $\frac{2}{3}$

3. $\frac{1}{3}$ **9.** $\frac{1}{2}$

4. $\frac{1}{5}$ **10.** $\frac{1}{3}$

5. $\frac{1}{7}$ **11.** $\frac{3}{8}$

6. $\frac{4}{5}$ **12.** $\frac{7}{12}$

B.

13. $\frac{1}{6} = \frac{6}{36}$ **18.** $\frac{3}{10} = \frac{15}{50}$

14. $\frac{5}{12} = \frac{20}{48}$ **19.** $\frac{1}{2} = \frac{5}{60}$

15. $\frac{1}{4} = \frac{7}{28}$ **20.** $\frac{1}{9} = \frac{6}{54}$

16. $\frac{3}{5} = \frac{24}{40}$ **21.** $\frac{7}{10} = \frac{21}{30}$

17. $\frac{5}{8} = \frac{20}{32}$

C.

22. **(5) $\frac{4}{5}$** If 12 out of 60 employees take the train, then 48 out of 60 drive. In lowest terms, 48 out of 60 is $\frac{4}{5}$.

23. **(2) 24 out of 72** If you write each item as a fraction and then reduce to lowest terms, only $\frac{24}{72}$ is equivalent to $\frac{1}{3}$.

24. **(2) Business B** Write each fraction with a common denominator of 24. The smallest fraction is $\frac{9}{24}$, which is $\frac{3}{8}$, or Business B.

FRACTIONS AND DECIMALS, PAGES 26–27

A.

1. $\frac{54}{100} = \frac{27}{50}$ **6.** $\frac{392}{1,000} = \frac{49}{125}$

2. $\frac{65}{100} = \frac{13}{20}$ **7.** $\frac{136}{1,000} = \frac{17}{125}$

3. $\frac{78}{100} = \frac{39}{50}$ **8.** $\frac{425}{1,000} = \frac{17}{40}$

4. $\frac{1}{10}$ **9.** $\frac{98}{100} = \frac{49}{50}$

5. $\frac{8}{100} = \frac{2}{25}$

B.

10. 0.15   **15.** 0.333

11. 0.9   **16.** 0.18

12. 0.6   **17.** 0.025

13. 0.417   **18.** 0.444

14. 0.533

C.

19. **(3) $10.20** The *ten* comes before the decimal point, and *twenty* cents is $0.20.

20. **(1) 5.24** For the mixed number $5\frac{6}{25}$, change $\frac{6}{25}$ to a decimal, which is 0.24.

21. **(5) It is less than $2\frac{1}{4}$ pounds.** The smallest number listed is $2\frac{1}{4}$. As a decimal, it is 2.25. Since 2.18 is less than 2.25, it is also less than all of the other numbers.

22. **(2) 0.84** Change the fractions to decimals, and then compare. $\frac{2}{3} = 0.6666$, and $\frac{3}{4} = 0.75$. The greatest number is 0.84, so this is the greatest distance.

ADD FRACTIONS, PAGES 28–29

A.

1. $\frac{4}{5}$

2. $\frac{5}{6}$ $\frac{4}{6} + \frac{1}{6} = \frac{5}{6}$

3. $\frac{7}{10}$ $\frac{3}{10} + \frac{4}{10} = \frac{7}{10}$

4. $\frac{5}{6}$ $\frac{4}{6} + \frac{1}{6} = \frac{5}{6}$

5. $\frac{11}{12}$ $\frac{6}{12} + \frac{5}{12} = \frac{11}{12}$

6. $\frac{7}{15}$ $\frac{5}{15} + \frac{2}{15} = \frac{7}{15}$

7. $\frac{4}{5}$ $\frac{8}{10} = \frac{4}{5}$

8. $\frac{5}{16}$ $\frac{3}{16} + \frac{2}{16} = \frac{5}{16}$

B.

9. $1\frac{1}{8}$ $\frac{6}{8} + \frac{3}{8} = \frac{9}{8} = 1\frac{1}{8}$

10. $1\frac{1}{6}$ $\frac{2}{6} + \frac{5}{6} = \frac{7}{8} = 1\frac{1}{6}$

11. $1\frac{5}{8}$ $\frac{7}{8} + \frac{2}{8} + \frac{4}{8} = \frac{13}{8} = 1\frac{5}{8}$

12. $1\frac{4}{5}$ $\frac{9}{5} = 1\frac{4}{5}$

13. $1\frac{5}{24}$ $\frac{20}{24} + \frac{9}{24} = \frac{29}{24} = 1\frac{5}{24}$

14. $1\frac{1}{6}$ $\frac{14}{12} = 1\frac{2}{12} = 1\frac{1}{6}$

C.

15. (3) $1\frac{19}{24}$ Find a common denominator and add.
$$\frac{18}{24} + \frac{9}{24} + \frac{16}{24} = \frac{43}{24} = 1\frac{19}{24}$$

16. (2) $2\frac{2}{5}$ First add $\frac{1}{2} + \frac{3}{10} = \frac{8}{10}$. Since Thomas does this 3 times, add $\frac{8}{10} + \frac{8}{10} + \frac{8}{10} = \frac{24}{10}$. Reduced to lowest terms, the total distance is $2\frac{4}{10}$, or $2\frac{2}{5}$ miles.

17. (3) $\frac{5}{12}$ Add the fractions for the Atkinson and Chester projects. $\frac{1}{6} + \frac{1}{4} = \frac{2}{12} + \frac{3}{12} = \frac{5}{12}$

SUBTRACT FRACTIONS, PAGES 30–31

A.

1. $\frac{1}{4}$ $\frac{2}{8} = \frac{1}{4}$

2. $\frac{3}{10}$ $\frac{9}{10} - \frac{6}{10} = \frac{3}{10}$

3. $\frac{1}{6}$ $\frac{5}{6} - \frac{4}{6} = \frac{1}{6}$

4. $\frac{2}{5}$ $\frac{4}{10} = \frac{2}{5}$

5. $\frac{3}{8}$ $\frac{6}{8} - \frac{3}{8} = \frac{3}{8}$

6. $\frac{1}{3}$ $\frac{11}{15} - \frac{6}{15} = \frac{5}{15} = \frac{1}{3}$

7. $\frac{1}{3}$ $\frac{4}{12} = \frac{1}{3}$

8. $\frac{11}{16}$ $\frac{13}{16} - \frac{2}{16} = \frac{11}{16}$

B.

9. $5\frac{3}{4}$ $9\frac{11}{8} - 4\frac{5}{8} = 5\frac{6}{8} = 5\frac{3}{4}$

10. $2\frac{5}{12}$ $12\frac{3}{12} - 9\frac{10}{12} = 11\frac{15}{12} - 9\frac{10}{12} = 2\frac{5}{12}$

11. $4\frac{5}{24}$ $4\frac{14}{24} - \frac{9}{24} = 4\frac{5}{24}$

12. $4\frac{1}{2}$ $8\frac{4}{10} - 3\frac{9}{10} = 7\frac{14}{10} - 3\frac{9}{10} = 4\frac{5}{10} = 4\frac{1}{2}$

C.

13. (4) $2\frac{7}{12}$ Express the mixed numbers with a common denominator, and then subtract.
$$8\frac{3}{4} - 6\frac{1}{6} = 8\frac{9}{12} - 6\frac{2}{12} = 2\frac{7}{12}$$

14. (1) **Mai's ride is $\frac{1}{6}$ hour longer.** Since 12 is a multiple of 4, express $\frac{1}{4}$ as an equivalent fraction with a denominator of 12. $\frac{1}{4} = \frac{3}{12}$, and $\frac{5}{12} - \frac{3}{12} = \frac{2}{12} = \frac{1}{6}$

15. (4) $\frac{1}{6}$ The amount in the recipe is $\frac{2}{3}$, so subtract $\frac{1}{2}$ from $\frac{2}{3}$ to find out how much more oil is needed.
$$\frac{2}{3} - \frac{1}{2} = \frac{4}{6} - \frac{3}{6} = \frac{1}{6}$$

MULTIPLY FRACTIONS, PAGES 32–33

A.

1. $\frac{9}{40}$

2. $\frac{8}{27}$

3. 21
$$\frac{3}{4} \times \overset{7}{\cancel{28}} = \frac{21}{1} = 21$$
(with 4 under the first fraction)

4. $\frac{3}{40}$

5. $\frac{3}{8}$
$$\overset{}{\cancel{6}} \times \overset{1}{\cancel{6}} = \frac{3}{8}$$
(with 2 and 4)

6. $\frac{1}{5}$
$$\frac{1}{\cancel{4}} \times \frac{\cancel{4}}{5} = \frac{1}{5}$$
(with 1)

7. 40

8. $\frac{5}{36}$
$$\frac{5}{\cancel{8}} \times \frac{\cancel{2}}{9} = \frac{5}{36}$$
(with 4)

9. $\frac{3}{50}$

B.

10. $2\frac{16}{25}$
$$\frac{\overset{2}{\cancel{4}}}{5} \times \frac{33}{\underset{5}{\cancel{10}}} = \frac{66}{25} = 2\frac{16}{25}$$

11. $14\frac{19}{20}$
$$\frac{\overset{13}{\cancel{26}}}{5} \times \frac{23}{\underset{4}{\cancel{8}}} = \frac{299}{20} = 14\frac{19}{20}$$

12. $2\frac{19}{36}$ $\frac{7}{12} \times \frac{13}{3} = \frac{91}{36} = 2\frac{19}{36}$

13. $4\frac{1}{16}$ $\frac{1}{2} \times \frac{65}{8} = \frac{65}{16} = 4\frac{1}{16}$

14. $11\frac{2}{3}$
$$\frac{5}{\cancel{4}} \times \frac{\overset{7}{\cancel{28}}}{3} = \frac{35}{3} = 11\frac{2}{3}$$
(with 1)

15. $4\frac{2}{9}$ $\frac{1}{3} \times \frac{38}{3} = \frac{38}{9} = 4\frac{2}{9}$

C.

16. (3) **150** Find the area by multiplying: $12\frac{1}{2} \times 16 = 200$ sq. ft. Then find $\frac{3}{4}$ of 200, which is 150 sq. ft.

17. (5) $\frac{1}{16}$ Half the cake is divided into 8 equal pieces, so each piece is $\frac{1}{8}$. To find the fraction of the original cake, multiply $\frac{1}{8}$ by $\frac{1}{2}$. $\frac{1}{8} \times \frac{1}{2} = \frac{1}{16}$

18. (2) $\frac{3}{4}$ To find $\frac{1}{3}$ of the amount of flour in the recipe, multiply $\frac{1}{3}$ by $2\frac{1}{4}$. $\frac{1}{3} \times \frac{9}{4} = \frac{3}{4}$

19. (2) $3\frac{1}{8}$ Multiply $\frac{1}{4}$ by the total weight of the meat.
$$\frac{1}{4} \times 12\frac{1}{2} = \frac{1}{4} \times \frac{25}{2} = \frac{25}{8} = 3\frac{1}{8}$$

DIVIDE FRACTIONS, PAGES 34–35

A.

1. 4 $\frac{2}{\cancel{8}} \times \frac{\overset{2}{\cancel{8}}}{1} = \frac{4}{1}$ (with 1)

2. $\frac{5}{6}$ $\frac{5}{\cancel{8}} \times \frac{\overset{1}{\cancel{4}}}{3} = \frac{5}{6}$ (with 2)

3. $\frac{7}{8}$ $\frac{7}{\cancel{12}} \times \frac{\overset{1}{\cancel{3}}}{2} = \frac{7}{8}$ (with 4)

4. $2\frac{2}{3}$ $\frac{4}{\cancel{8}} \times \frac{\overset{2}{\cancel{10}}}{3} = \frac{8}{3}$ (with 1)

5. $\frac{2}{3}$ $\frac{2}{\cancel{9}} \times \frac{\cancel{8}}{1} = \frac{2}{3}$ (with 3)

6. $3\frac{1}{2}$ $\frac{7}{\cancel{8}} \times \frac{\overset{1}{\cancel{4}}}{1} = \frac{7}{2} = 3\frac{1}{2}$ (with 2)

7. $1\frac{1}{10}$ $\frac{11}{\cancel{12}} \times \frac{\overset{1}{\cancel{6}}}{5} = \frac{11}{10} = 1\frac{1}{10}$ (with 2)

8. 5 $\frac{1}{\cancel{2}} \times \frac{\overset{5}{\cancel{10}}}{1} = \frac{5}{1} = 5$ (with 1)

9. $\frac{2}{3}$ $\frac{\overset{1}{\cancel{3}}}{\cancel{8}} \times \frac{\overset{2}{\cancel{10}}}{9} = \frac{2}{3}$ (with 1 and 3)

B.

10. 24 $\overset{3}{\cancel{6}} \times \dfrac{8}{\cancel{1}} = \dfrac{24}{1}$

11. $4\dfrac{1}{2}$ $\dfrac{\overset{9}{\cancel{27}}}{\underset{2}{\cancel{6}}} \times \dfrac{\cancel{4}}{\cancel{1}} = \dfrac{9}{2} = 4\dfrac{1}{2}$

12. $2\dfrac{9}{10}$ $\dfrac{\overset{29}{\cancel{87}}}{10} \times \dfrac{1}{\cancel{3}} = \dfrac{29}{10} = 2\dfrac{9}{10}$

13. $5\dfrac{19}{25}$ $24 \div \dfrac{25}{6} = 24 \times \dfrac{6}{25} = \dfrac{144}{25} = 5\dfrac{19}{25}$

14. $4\dfrac{14}{15}$ $\dfrac{37}{4} \div \dfrac{15}{8} = \dfrac{37}{15} \times \dfrac{\overset{2}{\cancel{8}}}{\cancel{4}} = \dfrac{74}{15} = 4\dfrac{14}{15}$

15. $10\dfrac{2}{3}$ $\dfrac{12}{1} \div \dfrac{9}{8} = \dfrac{\overset{4}{\cancel{12}}}{1} \times \dfrac{8}{\underset{3}{\cancel{9}}} = \dfrac{32}{3} = 10\dfrac{2}{3}$

C.

16. **(4) 15** Divide the height of the box by the book's width.
$13\dfrac{1}{8} \div \dfrac{7}{8} = \dfrac{105}{8} \times \dfrac{8}{7} = 15$

17. **(5) 18** Divide the width of the shelf by the width of the deck of cards.
$47\dfrac{1}{4} \div 2\dfrac{5}{8} = \dfrac{189}{4} \div \dfrac{21}{8} = \dfrac{189}{4} \times \dfrac{8}{21} = 18$

18. **(3) 6** Divide the width of the package by the measurement of the pencil.
$1\dfrac{1}{2} \div \dfrac{1}{4} = \dfrac{3}{2} \times 4 = 6$

19. **(2) 32** Divide the total weight of the meat by the amount of meat on each sandwich.
$24 \div \dfrac{3}{4} = 24 \times \dfrac{4}{3} = 32$

RATIOS, PAGES 36–37

A.

1. $\dfrac{2}{1}$ $\dfrac{64}{32} = \dfrac{2}{1}$ **6.** $\dfrac{32}{1}$ $\dfrac{64}{2} = \dfrac{32}{1}$

2. $\dfrac{3}{10}$ $\dfrac{30}{100} = \dfrac{3}{10}$ **7.** $\dfrac{4}{1}$ $\dfrac{16}{4} = \dfrac{4}{1}$

3. $\dfrac{\$3}{\$2}$ $\dfrac{\$150}{\$100} = \dfrac{\$3}{\$2}$ **8.** $\dfrac{5}{3}$ $\dfrac{500}{300} = \dfrac{5}{3}$

4. $\dfrac{4}{3}$ $\dfrac{8}{6} = \dfrac{4}{3}$ **9.** $\dfrac{3}{1}$ $\dfrac{15}{5} = \dfrac{3}{1}$

5. $\dfrac{7}{6}$ $\dfrac{14}{12} = \dfrac{7}{6}$ **10.** $\dfrac{5}{4}$ $\dfrac{40}{32} = \dfrac{5}{4}$

B.

11. $\dfrac{6 \text{ under age 20}}{45 \text{ age 20 and over}} = \dfrac{2}{15}$

12. $\dfrac{12 \text{ tulips}}{30 \text{ flowers}} = \dfrac{2}{5}$

13. $\dfrac{8 \text{ apples}}{18 \text{ pieces of fruit}} = \dfrac{4}{9}$

14. $\dfrac{4 \text{ blue}}{24 \text{ crayons}} = \dfrac{1}{6}$

C.

15. **(3) 10 calories to 3 grams fruit** The label shows 100 calories to 30 grams of fruit. Divide both numbers by 10 to write the reduced ratio 10 to 3.

16. **(2) $\dfrac{11}{15}$** The label shows 22 grams of carbohydrates for 30 grams of fruit. Divide both numbers by 2 to write the reduced the ratio $\dfrac{11}{15}$.

17. **(4) The Warriors outscored the Nets 4 to 1.** Since the Warriors scored more goals, they outscored the Nets. Write and reduce the ratio. 12 goals to 3 goals = 4 to 1

PROPORTIONS, PAGES 38–39

A.

1. $x = 75$ $30 \times \dfrac{100}{40} = \dfrac{3,000}{40} = 75$

2. $x = 8$ $7 \times \dfrac{64}{56} = \dfrac{448}{56} = 8$

3. $x = 16$ $2 \times \dfrac{24}{3} = \dfrac{48}{3} = 16$

4. $x = 15$ $12 \times \dfrac{40}{32} = \dfrac{480}{32} = 15$

5. $x = 70$ $10 \times \dfrac{49}{7} = \dfrac{490}{7} = 70$

6. $x = 15$ $19 \times \dfrac{60}{76} = \dfrac{1,140}{76} = 15$

7. $x = 105$ $21 \times \dfrac{40}{8} = \dfrac{840}{8} = 105$

8. $x = 3$ $4 \times \dfrac{36}{48} = \dfrac{144}{48} = 3$

9. $x = 320$ $40 \times \dfrac{88}{11} = \dfrac{3,520}{11} = 320$

10. $x = 7$ $35 \times \dfrac{9}{45} = \dfrac{315}{45} = 7$

11. $x = 66$ $3 \times \dfrac{110}{5} = \dfrac{330}{5} = 66$

12. $x = 8$ $4 \times \dfrac{36}{18} = \dfrac{144}{18} = 8$

B.

13. **6 minutes per mile** $\dfrac{4}{24} = \dfrac{1}{x}$; $24 \div 4 = 6$

14. **20 miles per gallon** $\dfrac{120}{6} = \dfrac{x}{1}$; $120 \div 6 = 20$

15. **\$225 per day** $\dfrac{1,125}{5} = \dfrac{x}{1}$; $1,125 \div 5 = 225$

16. **\$0.08 per ounce** $\dfrac{2.56}{32} = \dfrac{x}{1}$; $2.56 \div 32 = 0.08$

17. **20 people per group** $\dfrac{280}{14} = \dfrac{x}{1}$; $280 \div 14 = 20$

18. **\$6.75 per ticket** $\dfrac{33.75}{5} = \dfrac{x}{1}$; $33.75 \div 5 = 6.75$

C.

19. **(4) 5**
height $\dfrac{10 \text{ ft.}}{x} = \dfrac{1 \text{ ft.}}{0.5 \text{ in.}}$ $10 \times 0.5 = 5$ in.

20. **(4) $2\dfrac{1}{2}$**
$\dfrac{1 \text{ cup}}{4 \text{ servings}} = \dfrac{x \text{ cups}}{10 \text{ servings}}$ $\dfrac{1 \times 10}{4} = \dfrac{10}{4} = 2\dfrac{2}{4} = 2\dfrac{1}{2}$ cups

21. **(2) 47**
$\dfrac{6 \text{ students}}{1 \text{ teacher}} = \dfrac{282 \text{ students}}{x \text{ teachers}}$ $\dfrac{282}{6} = 47$ teachers

SOLVE FOR THE PART, PAGES 40–41

A.

1. base   **6.** base
2. part   **7.** base
3. rate   **8.** base
4. part   **9.** part
5. rate

B.

10. **314** $0.5 \times 628 = 314$
11. **126** $0.03 \times 4,200 = 126$
12. **27** $0.3 \times 90 = 27$
13. **70** $0.2 \times 350 = 70$
14. **1,980** $0.33 \times 6,000 = 1,980$
15. **62.5** $0.25 \times 250 = 62.5$
16. **9** $0.18 \times 50 = 9$
17. **88** $0.22 \times 400 = 88$

C.

18. **(4) 2,800** 56% of 5,000 = 0.56 × 5,000 = 2,800

19. **(4) 2,150** Romano has 2,800 votes. Gray has 13% of 5,000 = 0.13 × 5,000 = 650. Subtract: 2,800 − 650 = 2,150.

20. **(2) $40.80** Find 15% of $48.00 = 0.15 × 48 = $7.20. Subtract $7.20 from the regular price: $48.00 − $7.20 = $40.80.

21. **(3) $33.28** Find 8% of $416: 0.08 × 416 = 33.28

SOLVE FOR THE RATE, PAGES 42–43

A.

1. **6%** 15 ÷ 250 = 0.06 = 6%

2. **22%** 440 ÷ 2,000 = 0.22 = 22%

3. **15%** 30 ÷ 200 = 0.15 = 15%

4. **38%** 19 ÷ 50 = 0.38 = 38%

5. **75%** 6 ÷ 8 = 0.75 = 75%

6. **60%** 48 ÷ 80 = 0.6 = 60%

7. **5%** 20 ÷ 400 = 0.05 = 5%

8. **30%** 3.6 ÷ 12 = 0.3 = 30%

B.

9. **37.5%** 18 ÷ 48 = 0.375 = 37.5%

10. **90%** 9 ÷ 10 = 0.9 = 90%

11. **8%** 128 ÷ 1,600 = 0.08 = 8%

12. **42%** 420 ÷ 1,000 = 0.42 = 42%

13. **40%** 24 ÷ 60 = 0.4 = 40%

14. **35%** 28 ÷ 80 = 0.35 = 35%

15. **85%** 680 ÷ 800 = 0.85 = 85%

16. **10%** 1 ÷ 10 = 0.1 = 10%

C.

17. **(4) 55%** Add 33 dogs + 27 cats = 60 animals. Divide the part by the base: 33 ÷ 60 = 0.55 = 55%.

18. **(3) 8%** 4 out of 50 = 4 ÷ 50 = 0.08 = 8%

19. **(4) 30%** Add to find the total job cost, which is the base: 6,000 + 12,000 + 24,000 + 18,000 = 60,000. Divide the part by the base: 18,000 ÷ 60,000 = 0.3 = 30%.

SOLVE FOR THE BASE, PAGES 44–45

A.

1. **$35** 6.30 ÷ 0.18 = 35

2. **300** 96 ÷ 0.32 = 300

3. **250 lb.** 175 ÷ 0.7 = 250

4. **3,300** 1,485 ÷ 0.45 = 3,300

5. **$96** 48 ÷ 0.5 = 96

6. **62 kg** 15.5 ÷ 0.25 = 62

7. **120** 144 ÷ 1.2 = 120

8. **5,000** 3,400 ÷ 0.68 = 5,000

B.

9. **200%** 2,650 ÷ 1,325 = 2.00 = 200%

10. **75.4** 130% × 58 = 1.3 × 58 = 75.4

11. **90** 315 ÷ 350% = 315 ÷ 3.5 = 90

12. **$200** 230 ÷ 115% = 230 ÷ 1.15 = 200

13. **150%** 93 ÷ 62 = 1.5 = 150%

14. **$4,400** 220% × 2,000 = 2.2 × 2,000 = 4,400

15. **175%** 700 ÷ 400 = 1.75 = 175%

16. **136** 160% × 85 = 1.6 × 85 = 136

C.

17. **(4) 5,225** Divide the part (number who voted) by the rate (64%) to find the base (number of all registered voters). 3,344 ÷ 0.64 = 5,225

18. **(1) 3,344 ÷ 1.6** Divide the part (number of voters in this election) by the rate (160%, or 1.6) to find the base (number of voters in last election). Choice 2 shows the wrong formula. In choice 3, the percent was incorrectly changed to a whole number. Choices 4 and 5 use 5,225, which is the total number of registered voters, not the number who voted in this election.

19. **(2) $25.00** Divide the part (discount) by the rate (20%, or 0.2) to find the base (original price). $5.00 ÷ 0.2 = $25.

20. **(4) 135%** Divide the part (meals this month) by the base (meals last month) to find the rate. 8,910 ÷ 6,600 = 1.35 = 135%

PERCENT OF CHANGE, PAGES 46–47

A.

1. increase **3.** increase

2. decrease **4.** decrease

B.

5. **50% increase** 72 − 48 = 24, and 24 ÷ 48 = 0.5 = 50%

6. **80% decrease** 1,500 − 300 = 1,200, and 1,200 ÷ 1,500 = 0.8 = 80%

7. **50% decrease** 600 − 300 = 300, and 300 ÷ 600 = 0.5 = 50%

8. **60% increase** 3,200 − 2,000 = 1,200, and 1,200 ÷ 2,000 = 0.6 = 60%

9. **32% decrease** 250 − 170 = 80, and 80 ÷ 250 = 0.32 = 32%

10. **150% increase** 3,500 − 1,400 = 2,100, and 2,100 ÷ 1,400 = 1.5 = 150%

11. **30% increase** 2,340 − 1,800 = 540, and 540 ÷ 1,800 = 0.3 = 30%

12. **25% decrease** 840 − 630 = 210, and 210 ÷ 840 = 0.25 = 25%

13. **220% increase** 640 − 200 = 440, and 440 ÷ 200 = 2.2 = 220%

14. **10% decrease** 350 − 315 = 35, and 35 ÷ 350 = 0.1 = 10%

15. **75% decrease** 800 − 200 = 600, and 600 ÷ 800 = 0.75 = 75%

16. **4% increase** 26 − 25 = 1, and 1 ÷ 25 = 0.04 = 4%

C.

17. **(5) 15% increase** Subtract: 460 − 400 = 60. Then divide: 60 ÷ 400 = 0.15 = 15%. Since the new number is greater, it is an increase.

18. **(1) 70% decrease** Subtract: 120 − 36 = 84. Then divide: 84 ÷ 120 = 0.7 = 70%. Since the new number is less, it is a decrease.

19. **(5) 3.75% decrease** Subtract: $160,000 − $154,000 = $6,000. Then divide: $6,000 ÷ $160,000 = 0.0375 = 3.75%. Since the new price is lower, it is a decrease.

20. **(3) 110% increase** Subtract: 3,885 − 1,850 = 2,035. Then divide: 2,035 ÷ 1,850 = 1.1 = 110%. Since the new number is greater, it is an increase.

TABLES, PAGES 48–49

A.
1. lily leek and crocus
2. crocus
3. summer hyacinth
4. summer hyacinth and hardy amaryllis

B.
5. between 12:01 P.M. and 4:00 P.M.
6. 7 orders
7. 41 orders

C.
8. **(3) 14 hours 51 minutes** On day 3 sunrise is at 5:19 A.M. and sunset is at 8:10 P.M. From 5:19 P.M. to 8:19 P.M. is 15 hours. The time difference is 9 minutes less than this, or 14 hours 51 minutes.
9. **(4) 40%** Count the tally marks in the row for resort; there are 20. Find the total number of tally marks: 50. Divide to find the percent: $20 \div 50 = 0.4 = 40\%$.

MEAN, MEDIAN, AND MODE, PAGES 50–51

A.
1. mean, median, mode = 30
2. mean = 520, median = 524, mode = 524
3. mean = 81, median = 82, mode = 82
4. mean = $4.20, median = $4.25, mode = $4.25 and $4.40
5. mean = 8.2, median = 8.1, mode = 8.5
6. mean = 1,520; median = 1,500; mode = 1,500
7. mean = 228, median = 232.5, mode = 235
8. mean = 15, median = 14, mode = 12

B.
9. mean = $425, median = $425, mode = $415
10. mean = 32, median = 32, no mode
11. mean = 105, median = 104, mode = 102
12. mean = $180,400; median = $182,000; no mode

C.
13. **(3) 79** Write the numbers in order, and find the middle number: 77, 78, **79**, 80, 82.
14. **(5) $(77 + 79 + 82 + 80 + 78) \div 5$** To find the mean, add all of the heights, and divide by the number of items. Choices 1 and 4 show the incorrect operation with 5. Choice 2 divides by 4, but the number of items is 5. Choice 3 shows the correct sum but does not divide.
15. **(2) 158.4** Find the sum of the number of pages, and then divide by the number of books: $164 + 148 + 184 + 164 + 132 = 792$, and $792 \div 5 = 158.4$ pages.

BAR GRAPHS, PAGES 52–53

A.
1. 60 mph
2. Beltway
3. 15 mph faster
4. Route 2

B.
5. **operations** 10 men and 15 women
6. **13** 8 men + 5 women = 13
7. **3** 18 men − 15 women = 3
8. **71** 36 men + 35 women = 71

C.
9. **(3) 15** There are 10 clothing stores and 5 shoe stores. Add $10 + 5 = 15$, so 15 stores sell clothing or shoes.
10. **(4) This August is cooler than average.** There are fewer days above 90° and more days below 70° than average. You can conclude that temperatures are cooler than average. Choices 1, 2, and 5 deal with weather conditions that are not shown on this graph.

LINE GRAPHS, PAGES 54–55

A.
1. Between years 3 and 4 there was no increase in tuition.
2. $14,000
3. about $2,250
4. The tuition increased every year except from year 3 to year 4.

B.
5. May
6. $100
7. The checking account balance went down, then up, and then down. There does not appear to be a pattern.
8. The balance in the savings account will continue to increase each month.

C.
9. **(3) $14,800** The tuition continues to increase, but from year to year, the increase has not exceeded $800. Choices 1 and 2 have values that are less than the tuition for year 6. Choices 4 and 5 show increases greater than $5,000. They do not fit the trend.
10. **(2) $680** The savings account balance increases each month, usually between $50 and $100. Choice 2 fits with this trend. Choice 1 shows an amount that is less than the balance in June. Choices 3, 4, and 5 show increases of $200 or more, which do not match the trend.
11. **(5) A major employer has moved out of state.** This choice explains why people have left the town, causing the population to decrease. The other explanations offer reasons for people to move into town, causing the population to increase.

SCATTER PLOTS, PAGES 56–57

A.
1. negative correlation, strong
2. positive correlation, weak
3. negative correlation, weak
4. no correlation

B.
5. 48 inches
6. positive correlation, strong
7. As length increases, weight increases.
8. 45 inches

C.
9. **(5) positive correlation, strong** According to the scatter plot, as temperatures increase, the sales of air conditioners increase too. Since most points are very close to the fitted line, it is a strong correlation.
10. **(3) 18** Find 90° on the vertical axis, and then follow over to the line. It meets the line at about 18.

CIRCLE GRAPHS, PAGES 58–59

A.

1. **20%** $10 \div 50 = 0.2 = 20\%$
2. **Southeast and Southwest** $12 + 13 = 25$, and 25 is half of 50.
3. **0.14** $7 \div 50 = 0.14$
4. $\frac{4}{25}$ $\frac{8}{50} = \frac{4}{25}$

B.

5. **$332** Subtract take-home pay from gross pay: $800 - $468 = $332. Or add all deductions.
6. **8%** $64 \div 800 = 0.08 = 8\%$
7. **14%** $72 + 40 = 112$, $112 \div 800 = 0.14 = 14\%$
8. **12%** $96 \div 800 = 0.12 = 12\%$

C.

9. **(1) schools** The schools section is the largest, and 28% is the greatest percent.
10. **(5) $2,800** Find 28% of $10,000: $0.28 \times 10,000 = 2,800$.
11. **(3) $9,600** Together sports and recreation are 48% (23% + 25%). Find 48% of $20,000: $0.48 \times 20,000 = $9,600.

PROBABILITY, PART I, PAGES 60–61

A.

1. $\frac{3}{5}$
2. $\frac{1}{4}$
3. $\frac{5}{8}$
4. $\frac{2}{5}$

B.

5. $\frac{1}{5}$
6. $\frac{12}{25}$
7. $\frac{8}{25}$
8. $\frac{17}{25}$ If 16 trials are red, then $50 - 16 = 34$ trials are <u>not</u> red. So 34 out of 50, or $\frac{17}{25}$, are <u>not</u> red.

C.

9. **(3)** $\frac{1}{4}$ Of the 12 sections in the spinner, three are labeled with the number 1. 3 out of $12 = \frac{3}{12} = \frac{1}{4}$
10. **(2)** $\frac{1}{6}$ Two out of 12 sections are labeled with the number 2. $\frac{2}{12} = \frac{1}{6}$
11. **(4)** $\frac{3}{4}$ Since 3 out of 12 sections are labeled with the number 4, 9 out of 12 are <u>not</u> labeled with 4. $\frac{9}{12} = \frac{3}{4}$

PROBABILITY, PART II, PAGES 62–63

A.

1. dependent
2. independent
3. independent
4. dependent

B.

5. $\frac{1}{24}$ The probability of spinning blue is $\frac{1}{4}$. The probability of tossing a 6 is $\frac{1}{6}$. $\frac{1}{4} \times \frac{1}{6} = \frac{1}{24}$
6. $\frac{1}{16}$ The probability of spinning yellow is $\frac{1}{4}$, and $\frac{1}{4} \times \frac{1}{4} = \frac{1}{16}$.
7. $\frac{1}{4}$ The probability of tossing a number greater than 3 is $\frac{3}{6}$, or $\frac{1}{2}$. The probability of spinning yellow or green is $\frac{2}{4}$, or $\frac{1}{2}$. $\frac{1}{2} \times \frac{1}{2} = \frac{1}{4}$
8. $\frac{1}{9}$ The probability of tossing a 1 or 2 is $\frac{2}{6}$, or $\frac{1}{3}$. $\frac{1}{3} \times \frac{1}{3} = \frac{1}{9}$

C.

9. **(3)** $\frac{1}{49}$ After the first-prize ticket is picked, 49 tickets are left. The probability of any of these tickets being picked is 1 out of 49.
10. **(2)** $\frac{1}{13} \times \frac{1}{13}$ The probability of picking a 7 from a full deck of cards is $\frac{4}{52}$, or $\frac{1}{13}$. Multiply to find the probability of picking a 7 from both decks.
11. **(1)** $\frac{29}{330}$ Add to find the total number of tickets: $60 + 10 + 30 = 100$. The probability of picking a *20% off* card from the full box is $\frac{30}{100}$, or $\frac{3}{10}$. After that there are 99 tickets in the box, and 29 say 20% off, so the probability is $\frac{29}{99}$ for the second pick. Multiply both probabilities. $\frac{3}{10} \times \frac{29}{99} = \frac{29}{330}$

WORD PROBLEMS, PAGES 64–67
PAGE 65

1. Choice 5 is correct because the salad plus two extras costs $4.95 + $1.95 + $1.95 = $8.85.
2. Choice 2 is correct because you add the deposit and subtract the amount of the check: $465.28 + $600.00 − $275.13 = $790.15.

PAGES 66–67

1. **(1) 20%** Subtract the take-home pay from the gross pay to find the amount of deductions: $600 − $480 = $120. Then divide the deductions by the gross pay to calculate the percentage: $120 \div 600 = 0.2 = 20\%$.
2. **(3) F3** The wind speed (165) falls between 158 and 206, which fits within the F3 category.
3. **(2) $134.55** Find 10% of the purchase amount: $149.50 × 0.1 = $14.95. Then subtract the discount from the total purchase: $149.50 − $14.95 = $134.55.
4. **(4) $193.00** Multiply 5 years by 12 months per year to find the total number of payments (60). Divide the total cost by the number of payments to find the monthly payment: $11,580 \div 60 = $193.
5. **(5) Not enough information is given.** To solve, you need to know the weight of each kind of fruit.
6. **(3) 10% increase** Subtract to find the difference in profits: $88,000 − $80,000 = $8,000. Divide the difference by the original amount (last year's profit): $8,000 \div $80,000 = 0.1 = 10\%$. Since this year's profits are greater, the change is a 10% increase.
7. **(3) C, B, D, A** Compare the numbers on the folders, and write them in order from greatest to least: 4.2, 4.14, 4.02, 3.29. Then write the matching letters in the same order.
8. **(1) 12 to 1** The ratio of paid subscriptions to free subscriptions is 14,904 to 1,242. To write this ratio in lowest terms, divide both numbers by 1,242: $14,904 \div 1,242 = 12$ and $1,242 \div 1,242 = 1$.
9. **(5) 7.62** Multiply the weight of one jar by the total number of jars (6): $1.27 \times 6 = 7.62$ kg.
10. **(4) 0.488** Compare each number in the choices with 0.45 and 0.5. Only 0.488 is greater than 0.45 but less than 0.5.
11. **(3) $159.12** Multiply the number of gallons by the price per gallon: $122.4 \times $1.30 = $159.12.

12. **(5) Not enough information is given.** You cannot calculate the monthly payment without knowing the number of months Sheila will take to pay the remaining amount.

13. **(1) $\frac{7}{8}$** Multiply $\frac{1}{4}$ by the amount of paint $(3\frac{1}{2}$ gallons): $\frac{1}{4} \times 3\frac{1}{2} = \frac{1}{4} \times \frac{7}{2} = \frac{7}{8}$

PROBLEM SOLVING, PAGES 68–71
PAGE 69

1. Choice 5 is correct because 10 boxes of 24 books is $10 \times 24 = 240$, and 2 boxes of 8 books is $2 \times 8 = 16$. $240 + 16 = 256$

2. Choice 3 is correct because it shows that 6 full-time employees get $100 each and the 2 part-time employees each receive $50.

PAGES 70–71

1. **(3) ($2.49 ÷ 13) − ($3.29 ÷ 20)** To find the unit price, divide the price by the ounces for each box. Then subtract to find the difference.

2. **(5) $113.91** To find the cost of the purchase, add the prices: ($19.99 × 2) + $39.99 + $24.99 = $104.96. Since $104.96 is between $100.01 and $150.00, the shipping cost is $8.95. Add the shipping cost to find the total cost: $104.96 + $8.95 = $113.91.

3. **(1) (176 ÷ 22) × $1.85** Divide the distance (176 miles) by miles per gallon (22) to find the number of gallons needed to make the trip. Then multiply the number of gallons by the price per gallon ($1.85).

4. **(3) $9.00** Divide the price for a package of bags by the number of bags in the package to find the price for one bag: $7.50 ÷ 5 = $1.50. Then multiply the price by the number of bags used in a month: $1.50 × 6 = $9.00.

5. **(2) $16,160** Add all of the costs. $8,750 × 2 semesters = $17,500. $17,500 + $6,200 + $680 = $24,380. Subtract the amount of financial aid. $24,380 − $8,220 = $16,160.

6. **(3) 2:00 P.M. on Tuesday** Divide the distance by the speed to find the time: 450 ÷ 15 = 30 hours. Thirty hours later than 8:00 A.M. Monday is 2:00 P.M. on Tuesday.

7. **(2) 1.07 × $79 × 3** Multiply the nightly rate by the number of nights. ($79 × 3) The tax is 7%, or 0.07. You can multiply $79 × 3 × 1.07 to find the total with tax.

8. **(3) 9:10 A.M.** Add to find the total distance of the hike: 2.5 + 1.9 + 3.3 + 2.2 + 1.6 = 11.5 miles. Divide the distance by the rate (2 mph) to find the time: 11.5 ÷ 2 = 5.75, or 5 hours 45 minutes. Mark could leave by 9:10 A.M., at the latest.

9. **(4) $1,445** Add the charges for parts and labor to find the total cost: $545 + $1,200 = $1,745. Dale had to pay a $300 deductible, so subtract this amount from the total cost to find the amount the insurance company paid: $1,745 − $300 = $1,445.

10. **(1) $50 + $60 ×12** Add the deposit ($50) to the total monthly payments ($60 × 12 months).

11. **(3) $14.40** Multiply the length by the width to find the area of the room: 12 ft. × 8 ft. = 96 sq. ft. Then multiply 96 by each amount: 96 × $2.60 = $249.60, and 96 × $2.75 = $264.00. Subtract to find the difference: $264.00 − $249.60 = $14.40.

12. **(1) $0.74** Find the cost per issue for a 2-year subscription. Divide the subscription price by the number of issues: $66 ÷ 24 months = $2.75 per issue. Subtract this amount from the newsstand price to find the savings per issue: $3.49 − $2.75 = $0.74.

13. **(4) ($3,000 − $2,000 − $250) ÷ $2,000** The total amount spent on the car is the purchase price ($2,000) added to the amount spent for repairs ($250). To find the profit, subtract this sum from the selling price ($3,000). To find the percent the profit is of the original price, divide by the original purchase price ($2,000).

THE CASIO fx-260 CALCULATOR, PAGES 72–75
PAGE 73

1. Choice 4 is correct because you subtract the amount Stan was making from his current hourly wage to find the amount of the raise. $10.45 − $9.72 = $0.73

2. Choice 5 is correct because you add to find the total amount of ingredients. $2\frac{1}{4} + 1\frac{1}{3} = 3\frac{7}{12}$

PAGES 74–75

1. **(3) $5\frac{1}{4}$** Add to find the total time. $\frac{3}{4} + 4\frac{1}{2} = 5\frac{1}{4}$

2. **(4) 1.6 inches above average** Subtract the average rainfall from the amount for this June. 5.2 − 3.6 = 1.6. Since this June's amount is greater than the average, it is 1.6 inches above average.

3. **(2) $43.21** First, add the phone service and long-distance service: $54.23 + $1.48 = $55.71. Then subtract the savings amount: $55.71 − $12.50 = $43.21.

4. **(3) $7\frac{9}{10}$** Add the two lengths to find the total length of both roads: $3\frac{3}{10} + 4\frac{3}{5} = 7\frac{9}{10}$.

5. **(3) 38.4** Since the distance to work is 6.4 miles, the distance driven each day is 6.4 × 2, or 12.8 miles. Multiply the daily distance by the number of days: 12.8 × 3 = 38.4.

6. **(4) $16.77** Multiply the weight of the salmon (3.5 lb.) by the price per pound ($4.79): 3.5 × $4.79 = $16.77.

7. **(1) 46.28** Subtract 8 from the record time of 54.28: 54.28 − 8 = 46.28.

8. **(2) $8.56** Divide the amount of the gift ($25.68) by the number of people (3). $8.56 ÷ 3 = $8.56

9. **(2) $4,280.00** Ignore the fraction spent on materials. Multiply the total job cost by $\frac{1}{4}$. $17,120 × $\frac{1}{4}$ = $4,280

10. **(3) 5** Divide the total time of the concert by the time for each band: $2\frac{1}{2}$ hours ÷ $\frac{1}{2}$ hour = 5.

11. **(5) 3.91** Add the weight of each package to find the total weight: 1.38 + 1.24 + 1.29 = 3.91.

12. **(4) $3\frac{5}{8}$** Add the lengths of both cuts: $1\frac{1}{4} + 2\frac{3}{8} = 3\frac{5}{8}$.

13. **(2) $92\frac{3}{8}$** Subtract the length of the cuts from the original board length: 96 inches − $3\frac{5}{8}$ = $92\frac{3}{8}$.

14. **(4) 50** Find $\frac{5}{8}$ of 320 to learn the number of women employees: $\frac{5}{8} × 320 = 200$. Then find $\frac{1}{4}$ of 200 to learn the number of women managers: $\frac{1}{4} × 200 = 50$. You could also find $\frac{1}{4}$ of $\frac{5}{8}$ of the total workforce ($\frac{1}{4} × \frac{5}{8} = \frac{5}{32}$.) and multiply 320 by $\frac{5}{32}$ to find how many women managers there are.

THE STANDARD GRID, PAGES 76–79
PAGE 77

1. **229** Subtract the amount of the coupon from the price of the television: $249 − $20 = $229.

2. **4.6** Subtract the calories per minute for hiking from the calories per minute for jumping rope: 11.8 − 7.2 = 4.6.

PAGES 78–79

1. **3886** Multiply the price per person by the number of people: $58 × 67 = $3886.

2. **88** Divide the sum of the test scores by the number of scores: 86 + 89 + 79 + 94 + 87 + 93 = 528, and 528 ÷ 6 = 88.

3. **0.04** Divide the number of empty seats by the total number of seats: 20 ÷ 500 = 0.04.

4. **26** Find 8% of the unpaid balance: 0.08 × $325 = $26.

5. **504** Multiply the monthly cost by the number of months in a year: $42 × 12 = $504.

6. **1200** The tax rate is $12 per $1,000. The total property value is $100,000. Write and solve a proportion. $12/$1,000 = x/$100,000, so x = $1,200,000 ÷ $1,000 = $1,200

7. **8.83** The weight of the fruit is not needed to solve the problem, so ignore this information and add the prices. $1.88 + $2.20 + $4.75 = $8.83

8. **81.25** Divide the total price of the appliance by the number of equal payments: $975 ÷ 12 = $81.25.

9. **22.05** Multiply the price per line by the number of lines in the ad: $3.15 × 7 = $22.05.

10. **360** Divide the total distance by the number of days: 1,080 ÷ 3 = 360 miles per day.

11. **412.5** Multiply the price per square foot by the number of square feet: $1.50 × 275 = $412.50. Note that the end zero must be omitted to fit on the grid.

12. **892** Add the number of each type of member: 358 + 289 + 245 = 892.

13. **15** Divide the total number of players by the number of players needed for each team: 180 ÷ 12 = 15.

14. **48.2** Subtract the mile markers: 125 − 76.8 = 48.2 miles away.

15. **743** Add the number of each kind of fish stocked: 240 + 315 + 188 = 743.

FRACTIONS ON THE STANDARD GRID, PAGES 80–83
PAGE 81

1. **1/4** Write a fraction and express it in lowest terms: 8 out of 32 = $\frac{8}{32} = \frac{1}{4}$.

2. **35/8** Since the answer has to be recorded as an improper fraction, first change the mixed number to an improper fraction and then divide by 2: $8\frac{3}{4} = \frac{35}{4}$, and $\frac{35}{4} \div 2 = \frac{35}{4} \times \frac{1}{2} = \frac{35}{8}$.

PAGES 82–83

1. **4/5** First, add to find the total number of games: 48 + 10 + 2 = 60. Then write a fraction comparing games won to total number of games: $\frac{48}{60} = \frac{4}{5}$.

2. **13/12** Use a common denominator of 12: $\frac{3}{4} = \frac{9}{12}$, and $\frac{1}{3} = \frac{4}{12}$.
Then add the fractions: $\frac{9}{12} + \frac{4}{12} = \frac{13}{12}$.

3. **1/10** Since 36 out of 40 tables are occupied, 4 out of 40 are available. $\frac{4}{40} = \frac{1}{10}$

4. **3/2** Divide the height of the stack by the number of cans to find the height of each can: $12 \div 8 = \frac{12}{8} = \frac{3}{2}$.

5. **3/5** Add to find the total number of DVDs: 60 + 18 + 12 + 10 = 100. Then find the fraction of the total that are comedies: $\frac{60}{100} = \frac{3}{5}$.

6. **7/10** If Julia spent $15, then she has $50 − $15, or $35 left on the gift card. Write a fraction comparing the amount she has left with the original value of the gift card: $\frac{35}{50} = \frac{7}{10}$.

7. **5/2** Divide the number of gallons used for the trip by the number of gallons the gas tank holds: $40 \div 16 = 2\frac{1}{2}$. Then change the mixed number to an improper fraction: $2\frac{1}{2} = \frac{5}{2}$.

8. **21/2** If the board is cut in half, each piece will measure $3\frac{1}{2}$ ft. by 3 ft. To find the area of each half, multiply $3\frac{1}{2}$ by 3. $3\frac{1}{2} \times 3 = \frac{7}{2} \times \frac{3}{1} = \frac{21}{2}$

9. **8/3** Add the amounts for each kind of vegetable: $1\frac{1}{2} + \frac{2}{3} + \frac{1}{2} = 2\frac{2}{3}$. Then express as an improper fraction: $2\frac{2}{3} = \frac{8}{3}$.

10. **1/2** $\frac{3}{4}$ of $\frac{2}{3}$ of the respondents chose Brand A but regularly buy Brand B. Multiply the fractions: $\frac{3}{4} \times \frac{2}{3} = \frac{1}{2}$.

11. **9/4** Subtract to find the difference in height between the two plants: $38\frac{3}{4} − 36\frac{1}{2} = 2\frac{1}{4}$. Write the difference as an improper fraction: $2\frac{1}{4} = \frac{9}{4}$.

12. **9/2** Multiply the amount of material needed for each bag by the number of bags in the order: $\frac{3}{4} \times 6 = \frac{18}{4} = \frac{9}{2}$.

13. **7/12** Add the fractions shown in the graph for radio and newspaper ads: $\frac{1}{4} + \frac{1}{3} = \frac{3}{12} + \frac{4}{12} = \frac{7}{12}$.

14. **1/6** Subtract the fraction for television ads from the fraction for radio ads: $\frac{1}{4} − \frac{1}{12} = \frac{3}{12} − \frac{1}{12} = \frac{2}{12} = \frac{1}{6}$.